The Mystery of James Revealed in Droplets of Grace

Mac Goddard

iUniverse, Inc.
Bloomington

iUniverse books may be ordered through booksellers or by contacting:

iUniverse
1663 Liberty Drive
Bloomington, IN 47403
www.iuniverse.com
1-800-Authors (1-800-288-4677)
ISBN: 978-1-4759-2573-9 (sc)
ISBN: 978-1-4759-2574-6 (e)
ISBN: 978-1-4759-2575-3 (dj)

Library of Congress Control Number: 2012908417

Printed in the United States of America

iUniverse rev. date: 05/23/2012

Contents

Preface

As you can tell from the table of contents, there are thirty-one chapters in this small book, and that is not without purpose. It is my intention that you read this, not as a book, per se, but as daily food for thought. Begin by reading the chapter that corresponds with the day of the month, and continue on a daily basis until you complete the book. You will probably be surprised to learn just how timely the daily messages are in your walk with Him.

Introduction

Thankfully, my father made it home alive and well from World War II and not in one of those boxes that became all too familiar to me in the years to come, when I worked as a mortician.

In the providence of God, Daddy and Mama settled in his hometown—Reynolds, Georgia, population twelve hundred—where they would spend the rest of their lives (population still twelve hundred). Somewhere in 1947, Mama trusted Jesus to be her Savior, which meant that life for her and for her family would never be the same—not even close.

I am confident that what Mama went through during Daddy's service in the navy motivated her to learn to pray, and pray she did—every day. She was known as a "prayer warrior!" As a result of her prayer life, she became a lover of the scriptures.

Soon after her conversion experience, she realized the importance of praying for her firstborn, specifically that he would trust that same Jesus to be his Savior. In August 1948 her prayers were answered. As a result of that experience and watching her pray and read the Bible, I, too, became a lover of Holy Writ. Thankfully, I have spent most of the past sixty-plus years studying the scriptures, not just to gain head knowledge, but to know Him whom to know is eternal life.

Interestingly, in the early days of my study, the book that gave me the most difficulty was the book of James. Even Martin Luther, the iconic figure of the Protestant Reformation, in his introduction to the first edition of his German New Testament [1522], called it "a right strawy epistle," so I suppose I was in good company. Unfortunately, I was attempting to understand it through the lenses of the law—legalism; consequently, it nearly killed me. I simply could not put it into practice, and I, certainly, could not make it fit into the writings of Jesus and Paul. At almost every turn, James seemed to contradict what they believed.

Later on in my journey, I began to read and, consequently, to understand it through the lenses of grace, and, ever so slowly, I began to have a measure of clarity. What you hold in your hand represents years of prayer and study. It is, for lack of a better explanation, my perspective of this incredible book. It is my sincere prayer that the Holy Spirit will allow you to find the needle of truth that will give you clarity regarding this haystack of Holy Writ.

1

When You Encounter Various Trials

"Consider it all joy, my brethren, when you encounter various trials, knowing that the testing of your faith produces endurance. And let endurance have its perfect result, that you may be perfect and complete, lacking in nothing. But if any of you lacks wisdom, let him ask of God, who gives to all men generously and without reproach, and it will be given to him. But let him ask in faith without doubting, for the one who doubts is like the surf of the sea driven and tossed by the wind. For let not that man expect that he will receive anything from the Lord, being a double-minded man, unstable in all his ways" (James 1:2–8).

Typically, when we encounter various trials, what we want is relief—quick relief; however, James tells us to consider it all joy, when we encounter trials. His reason is as follows: the trials are God's way of testing our faith and, thereby, producing the quality of endurance.

As I contemplate this, it becomes obvious to me that God deems it very important that the quality of endurance be developed within our lives. It becomes just as obvious that He knows that we will never develop it on our own because our desire for relief is so much greater than our desire for developing endurance. He is well aware that we will do anything to avoid adversity, even the slightest adversity. Consequently, He intervenes by placing trials into our lives, trials from which we cannot escape until our faith has been proven and the fruit of endurance blossoms forth, fruit that, according to James, somehow enables us to be perfect and complete, lacking nothing.

Now, based on what the rest of the scriptures teach us regarding the doctrine of soteriology (salvation), I must assume that the "perfect and complete" to which James refers has nothing to do with the finished work of Jesus, by which He justified us and sanctified us, thereby making us perfect and complete before God. Surely, endurance cannot accomplish what it took the vicarious death, burial, and resurrection of Jesus to accomplish! This assumption, however, leaves us with this obvious question: if James's reference to our being "perfect and complete" has nothing to do with our standing before God, then to what is he referring?

In my opinion, James is referring to our becoming mature as Christians; however, this maturity has nothing to do with how often we have a quiet time, or how quickly we forgive, or how quickly we turn the other cheek, or how generously we give, or how infrequently we curse, or how much better we are this year than we were last year. Much to the contrary, this maturity has to do with our ability to exercise the measure of faith that God has so graciously entrusted to us, a measure of faith that is evidenced by our trusting Him (resting in His finished work) when we are traveling through the worst of trials. In the end, this makes it quite clear that not one of us is fully mature, not even close; consequently, we can expect the trials to continue until we perfectly and completely trust Him in every situation and circumstance.

Notice that to his "perfect and complete" he adds, "lacking in nothing." Again, James cannot be referring to something we lack regarding our justification, sanctification, or glorification. Our lacking something (anything) would reduce the significance of the death, burial, resurrection, and ascension of Jesus to an equal significance with the Law of Moses. In other words, the gospel message would be essentially this: something is lacking in your life, and that "something" separates you from God and prevents you from being in right standing with Him. Be encouraged, however, because God is going to give you many chances (opportunities) to obtain it by leading you into various trials, trials that will either prove or disprove your faith. If you go through the various trials correctly and, thereby, prove your faith, then you will be perfect and complete, lacking in nothing! Surely, we can all readily see that this would *not* be good news, but the worst news ever reported! This would be the epitome of legalism! We are, however, once again left with the obvious question: to what is James referring when he mentions our "lacking in nothing"?

If the chief end of the "testing of our faith" is the fruit of endurance, endurance that produces maturity, then surely his reference to our "lacking in nothing" has to do with our becoming mature as believers, not to Jesus's work being incomplete! I might add that, within the context of our passage, it seems that what we lack most as we experience these various trials is wisdom—His wisdom.

You see, most of us *react* to the various trials that come our way, and our reactions are based on the self-centered wisdom of man, not on the wisdom of God. Consequently, our reactions serve only to prolong the various trials. I have to believe that were our responses to these trials based on the wisdom of God, the fruit of endurance would be born much more quickly than it would be otherwise.

Interestingly, according to James, this wisdom that comes from God is readily available to each one of us. Apparently, all that is necessary for our receiving a "heaping helping" of it is our asking for it, with this one stipulation: we must not doubt that God will give it to us. James makes it very clear that the man who doubts is like the surf of the sea driven and tossed by the wind, that he is a man with a mind and a mind—a double-minded man—who is unstable in all his ways. Furthermore, this man, according to James, should not expect to receive anything from the Lord.

I do not know about you, but this would easily and readily overwhelm me (or cause me to pretend), were it not for the fact that I know a secret. I think the next two verses shed much light on this secret, even expose it: "But let the brother of humble circumstances glory in his high position; and let the rich man glory in his humiliation, because like flowering grass he will pass away" (James 1:9–10). To be honest, I am not sure that James even realized it, but our only hope of having the faith to believe that God will give us His wisdom is admitting our helplessness to gain it on our own and our desperate need for Him to send Jesus to rescue us.

In a message that Francis Jackson, a pastor from India, preached several years ago at Grace Christian Fellowship, the church I pastor, he made it abundantly clear that God is a God of miracles, and he encouraged us to expect a miracle, and to expect it that day. As he preached, I wondered just what kind of miracle each of us might have been expecting. If my guess were correct, then most (probably all) of us were expecting a miracle that would bring what we perceived to be much-needed relief from one of the various trials to which James refers. I feel confident that the development of endurance was not nearly as high on our list as was relief!

Having said that, allow me to make another guess: although many of the folk left the service truly expecting a miracle, it has not yet taken place. If you will be honest, you will have to admit that this has happened to you many times. If you will be even more honest, you will also admit that the disappointment has happened so many times that you would be completely surprised if the miracle you expected (relief) actually happened.

As Brother Francis continued his message, it became obvious that each of the three illustrations he gave to us (the raising of the widow of Nain's son; the raising of Mary and Martha's brother, Lazarus; and the raising of Jairus's daughter) had something in common other than the miracle of resurrection, and that commonality is this: the miracle of Jesus's presence! To be sure, God chose to bring the much-wanted relief to these grieving loved ones; however, not without the presence of Jesus.

Yes, these grieving people were asking for relief, not for Jesus, and for reasons beyond me, God chose to give them the relief they wanted (maybe endurance had been born within each of their lives). In all probability, each one of us has experienced the miracle of relief and been very grateful for it; however, I wonder what would happen if we stopped expecting or demanding the miracle of relief, and began to cry out for the miracle of Jesus's presence. I have to believe that the miracle of His presence is *always* better than the miracle of relief.

When He shows up, nothing else matters! It seems to me that when the cry of our heart is for His presence and not for mere relief, endurance has accomplished its perfect work, and spiritual maturity is well on its way.

2
The Crown of Life

> "Blessed is a man who perseveres under trial; for once he has been approved, he will receive the crown of life, which the Lord has promised to those who love Him" (James 1:12).

Like many passages in James, at first glance this one appears to be very contradictory to the message of the gospel because it implies that one's receiving the crown of life depends upon his ability to persevere under trial. In other words, a casual reading of this passage would indicate that God has promised the crown of life to those who love Him; however, there is this stipulation: the recipient must have proved his worthiness by demonstrating his ability to persevere under trial. In my opinion, this is one of the reasons Martin Luther took such offense at James's writing, calling it "strawy." To be sure, this is a very legalistic view of the passage.

Because, like Luther, I am certain that the crown of life God has promised those He loves is not something *achieved* but rather a gift *received*, I want us to take a more careful look at this text.

In the first place, the word for "crown" in this passage refers to the wreath that was placed on the victor's head in athletic events, a wreath that *symbolized* persevering triumph, not the crown of royalty. I make this distinction because we are prone to reverse the roles and, thereby, to make God the victim of our shenanigans. We are the runners in the race, not God! Make no mistake: we are, indeed, born again with His royal blood flowing through our veins; however, this is a thing of grace and mercy, not a thing we earn by persevering.

In the second place, if there is a test we must pass (as James indicates) in order to receive the crown of life and, if that test has to do with our ability to persevere under trial (*unless* failing is passing), none of us will ever receive the crown of life. If there is some kind of race we must win, by and through our own ability to persevere, we are all losers, *unless* the winners are the ones who are unable to finish on their own.

In the third place, if this "crown of life" is something we wear as evidence of our having passed the test of perseverance, it is a crown of self-righteousness and, consequently, it is despicable to God. One of the foundation stones of the gospel is that our righteousness is as filthy rags before God (Isaiah 64:6); consequently, you can rest assured that He has made no exception in this text.

In the fourth place, James indicates that God blesses the man who perseveres under trial, and within context of our text, the major pieces of this blessing are God's approval and the crown of life. Realizing that the crown of life to which James refers is eternal life, these blessings become all the more important—crucially and critically important. You see, if we are not careful to truly understand what James is saying, we will hinge the gift of God's approval and the gift of eternal life on our own filthy rags, which would be a terrible mistake. Let us, however, not make that terrible mistake, since we know that both God's approval of us and our eternal life hinge upon the finished work of Jesus—nothing more, nothing less. That is the heart and essence of the gospel of grace.

Finally, the text indicates that this crown of life is promised to those who love God. James, however, makes it appear that God only loves those who pass the test of perseverance, as is evidenced by the fact that these are the ones He rewards with His approval and the crown of life. Again, one of the foundation stones of the gospel is that our receiving both God's approval and His love does not depend on our desiring them or pursuing them, but on God, who has mercy. "So then it does not depend on the man who wills or the man who runs, but on God who has mercy" (Romans 9:16). In other words, God's love toward us is in no way dependent upon anything we might or might not do; instead, it depends upon His sovereign choice.

Having made my case to affirm Martin Luther's belief that the book of James is a bit "strawy," I want to proceed with what I believe is the "meat and potatoes" of this passage. Since the book of James is a part of the canon of scripture, we must seek to find the truth in this passage and, somehow, connect it to the New Covenant. I am very confident that James did not intend to contradict the very teachings for which his half brother, Jesus, lived and died.

First, the man who perseveres under trial is, indeed, a blessed man because the much-needed quality of endurance is being developed within his life, the quality that promotes his Christian maturity. The scriptures contain many examples— Noah, Moses, Abraham, Habakkuk, Stephen, Paul, and Peter, to name a few. However, we must understand that their ability to persevere (endure) during such extreme trial (adversity) had nothing to do with *them* and all to do with *Him*. Again, this is the heart and essence of the gospel of grace.

Without exception, these men had been handpicked and empowered by God to make very specific and significant journeys. Take Paul, for example: "Go, for he is a chosen instrument of Mine, to bear My name before the Gentiles and kings and the sons of Israel; for I will show him how much he must suffer for My name's sake" (Acts 9:15–16). There can be no mistaking that Paul had been handpicked by God to carry out a specific purpose, and *that* not without suffering (adversity, trial), even intense suffering.

Surely, we do not think, even for a minute, that God sent Paul out *on his own* to prove his ability to persevere under trial and, thereby, to receive His approval, along with the crown of life! How would this man, who was accustomed to having everything he wanted, who was used to living the lifestyle of "Mr. Israel," ever persevere under such intense suffering (imprisoned, beaten times without number, lashed with thirty-nine lashes five times, beaten with rods, stoned, shipwrecked, left a night and a day in the deep, ad infinitum)? Acts 9:17 gives us the clue we need: "Brother Saul, the Lord Jesus, who appeared to you on the road by which you were coming, has sent me so that you may regain your sight, and be filled with the Holy Spirit." You see, Jesus, in the person of the Holy Spirit, was Paul's guarantee of persevering, even to the end!

I am convinced that Paul was approved, and that he received the crown of life; however, it was the result of His doing, not his doing! It was the result of God's sovereign choice to empower him with the Holy Spirit, not as the result of his abilities to persevere under trial.

Second, the aforesaid being the *meat* and this being the *potatoes:* the crown of life is not something we are given to wear as some adornment; instead, it is something we humbly lay at the feet of the One who deserves it—Jesus! We must never forget that this is about Him and not about us! It is about Jesus being glorified in what He has accomplished on our behalf! It is about His receiving all of the attention, as we humbly rejoice and lift praises to Him!

We must never forget that had God not chosen to give us that which we could have never earned, we would be helpless, hopeless, and damned to an eternal hell. To be sure, we would have never passed the test of perseverance, much less would we have received His approval, and, therefore, certainly not the crown of life!

In conclusion, it is certain that those who love God, who have received His approval, and who have been given eternal life will persevere under any and all trials, and it is also certain that we will persevere until the very end. The perseverance of the saints is certain because Jesus is our guarantee of persevering; however, the wreath we wear, the victor's crown, is evidence of His strength and faithfulness, not ours! May He be blessed forever! Amen!

3

Temptation

"Let no one say when he is tempted, "I am being tempted by God"; for God cannot be tempted by evil, and He Himself does not tempt anyone. But each one is tempted when he is carried away and enticed by his own lust. Then when lust has conceived, it brings forth sin; and when sin is accomplished, it brings forth death" (James 1:13–15).

Within the context of this text, to be tempted is to be enticed through deception to do something that is evil, sinful. Obviously, each one of us has plenty of experience in this arena; consequently, temptation is no stranger to us. Unfortunately, however, we all seem to be slow learners, as is evidenced by our poor success rate at overcoming temptation.

Interestingly, James does not address overcoming temptation in this text; instead, he gives us a twofold warning: (1) he warns us not to blame God for our being tempted, and (2) he warns us to realize that we are inviting temptation when we allow ourselves to be carried away and enticed by our own lust.

In light of its use in this text, I think it is important to note that "lust" is not always associated with evil. A brief look at a few of its synonyms (yearn for, desire, long for, hunger for, ache for) should help to correct this misconception. Obviously, one can yearn (lust) for Jesus, even ache (lust) for Him, neither of which is associated with evil. In our text, however, James is addressing our lusting for that which is evil, specifically, our being enticed and carried away by this lust and, thereby, being tempted to do evil.

Having said that, let us follow James's logic:

1. He makes it clear that we will be tempted to do evil, by his choice of "when" not "if" in verse 13 (*Let no one say when he is tempted*).
2. We should never blame God for our being tempted with evil because God cannot be tempted by evil and, consequently, He does not tempt anyone with evil.
3. When we are tempted with evil it is because we are being carried away and enticed by our own lust.
4. When lust has conceived, it gives birth to sin.
5. When sin is accomplished, it brings forth death.

On the one hand, this means that every believer will continuously be tempted with evil. As I am sure you know, evil is oftentimes much more attractive to us than righteousness; consequently, we are easily carried away and enticed by it. On the other hand, it means that God is never tempted with evil because He *never* finds it appealing or attractive; consequently, He is never carried away or enticed by it. Obviously, He will never tempt us to do that which He finds offensive. By virtue of His nature, He cannot tempt us with evil!

Now for the biggie: one is tempted (with evil) when he is carried away and enticed by his own lust; however, when that lust is conceived, it gives birth to sin, and when sin is accomplished (i.e., when sin gets a foothold), it gives birth to death! I like the way the author of *The Message*[1] translates it: *Lust*

1 Eugene H. Peterson, *The Message* (Colorado Springs, CO: Nav-Press, 2002), 2,202.

gets pregnant, and has a baby: sin! Sin grows up to adulthood, and becomes a real killer.

To be sure, the temptation to commit evil comes our way often, and when it comes, it does so as the result of our being carried away and enticed by our own lust. However, we must not conclude that lust and temptation are sin, at least not in and of themselves. As James sees it, sin enters the picture only when lust conceives.

Think before you reject! If lust and temptation fall into the category of sin, we must label Jesus as a sinner because He was tempted in all things, just as we are. We often forget that He was an authentic man, one who chose to live among us and to be tempted in all things, just as we are tempted. Admittedly and thankfully, there is this one significant difference: He never allowed His own lust to conceive; consequently, it never gave birth to sin! "For we do not have a high priest who cannot sympathize with our weaknesses, but one who has been tempted in all things as we are, yet without sin" (Hebrews 4:15).

Take heart! It really is okay to be human, and it is okay that your lust is so powerful that you find yourself "carried away and enticed"—tempted! It is even okay if your lust conceives and gives birth to sin! The truth is it has already done so, and God still forgives you, accepts you, and loves you! Thankfully, God forgives *and* forgets.

Now do not misunderstand me! I did not say that sin is okay. What I said is this: as a believer, you are okay, even when your lust conceives and gives birth to sin, and you are because of the finished work of Jesus. Obviously, were it not true that God already forgives you, accepts you, and loves you unconditionally, you would have no desire for Jesus; instead, you would be dancing merrily along in your own self-righteousness.

What is not okay, however, is thinking you can handle your own lust! The moment you buy into that lie, buzzards begin to circle. The story of David is a very good example. Turn to 2 Samuel 11 and read his story. I think you will see what I mean. It was quite normal for him to have been tempted when he saw Bathsheba bathing; after all, he was alive. Furthermore, it was quite normal for him to have allowed himself to be "carried away and enticed"—tempted! Who could fault him? I am going even a step further and saying that, although his lust did conceive and give birth to sin, God continued to see him as a man after His own heart![2]

The fact is sinners sin; however, nothing can separate us from the love of God—nothing! Yes (for the skeptics), there were consequences, severe consequences; however, they were *not* designed to destroy David but to bring him into a deeper intimacy with God than he would, otherwise, have ever known.

To be sure, David found himself in a rather difficult place; however, I am not so sure that we understand why. I really do not think it had as much to do with the sins of adultery, lying, murder, and deception, as it had to do with David's thinking he could manage his own lust. You can count on this: the moment David bought into that lie, the buzzards started circling and, I might add, they were not circling for Uriah!

You see, lust "conceives" the moment we think we can manage (control) it, and when it conceives, it brings forth sin— much sin! I can tell you that it brought forth much more sin for David than he ever bargained for, and that is for sure. From the moment he saw Bathsheba bathing, he was convinced that he could handle his own lust. In his mind, he was convinced that this "peep" would never develop into anything of consequence. As you know, he was wrong, and from that point forward, things went downhill and very quickly!

Fortunately, we have another example, one that turns out quite a bit differently. Turn to Matthew 4 and read the story of Jesus's experience on the Mount of Temptation. No! He was not

2 1 Samuel 13:14; Acts 13:22.

peeping over a fence watching a woman bathe! His plight was much more difficult. He had just finished a fast of forty days and nights and, as you can imagine, He was hungry. As He stood atop this mountain—mountain man hungry—gazing at the vast wilderness of rocks and stones below, all of a sudden, He was "carried away and enticed"—tempted!—as each of the stones began to look like freshly baked loaves of bread. Of course, He knew the stones were not bread; however, He also knew that *He could* turn them into bread, freshly baked loaves of bread, simply by speaking it so. You know the story. You know that Jesus refused to allow His own lust to conceive; instead, He quoted from the Bread of Life and, thereby, satisfied His hunger. "It is written, 'Man shall not live by bread alone, but on every word that proceeds out of the mouth of God'" (Matthew 4:4).

Can you see the difference in the way David and Jesus responded to temptation? It should be obvious: Jesus knew that He could not manage His own temptation and, therefore, turned to the One who could and would do it for Him. Maybe, just maybe, we could all learn from Jesus! What do you think?

4

Sin Brings Forth Death

"Let no one say when he is tempted, 'I am being tempted by God'; for God cannot be tempted by evil, and He Himself does not tempt anyone. But each one is tempted when he is carried away and enticed by his own lust. Then when lust has conceived, it brings forth sin; and when sin is accomplished, it brings forth death" (James 1:13–15).

James's assertion that when sin is accomplished it brings forth death, is a prime example of why Luther labeled James as a book of straw, having no relationship to the gospel, and that it should have no place in the canon of scriptures. The fact, however, is that this book *is* included in the scriptures, so we must treat it as such.

If we are going to attempt to reconcile this portion of our text with the writing of Jesus and Paul, then we must assume that James is not referring to spiritual death, at least not for the believer. To be sure, Adam's sin resulted in death, both physical and spiritual death; in fact, it resulted in death for all men. "Therefore, just as through one man sin entered into the world, and death through sin, and so death spread to all men, because all sinned" (Romans 5:12). Thankfully, however, believers do have a Redeemer—Jesus!

Yes, there are those who teach that believers can sin (usually they identify it as a grave sin, as if some are not) and lose their salvation and thus die spiritually. However, that position leaves much to be desired regarding the efficacy of the blood of Jesus, and it certainly does not say much about those passages that inform us that Jesus took our sins away, never to remember them again. "'This is the covenant that I will make with them after those days,' says the Lord: 'I will put My laws upon their heart, and upon their mind I will write them.' He then says, 'And their sins and their lawless deeds I will remember no more'" (Hebrews 10:16–17).

If you are one of those who believes that you, as a believer, can die for some sin you might commit (or might have committed, for that matter), consider this: "And when you were dead in your transgressions and the uncircumcision of your flesh, He made you alive together with Him, having forgiven us all our transgressions, having canceled out the certificate of debt consisting of decrees against us and which was hostile to us; and He has taken it out of the way, having nailed it to the cross" (Colossians 2:13–14).

To be sure, there are sins that can lead to physical death—many of them. For example, you could get caught committing adultery with another man's wife and that man could shoot you dead. However, if you are a believer, (i.e., if Jesus is your redeemer), then that sin cannot lead to your spiritual death. He died spiritually—separated from God—so that you would not have to.

Now, please do not assume that I am implying that sin is not a serious matter because it is—very serious. As a matter of fact, it is so serious that Jesus had to die in order to purchase for us a clean record before God.

I think Jesus put this to rest with these words: "My sheep hear My voice, and I know them, and they follow Me; and I give eternal life to them, and they shall never perish; and no one shall snatch them out of My hand. My Father, who has given them to Me, is greater than all; and no one is able to snatch them out of the Father's hand. I and the Father are one" (John 10:27–30).

5

Dealing with Change

> "Every good thing bestowed and every perfect gift is from above, coming down from the Father of lights, with whom there is no variation, or shifting shadow" (James 1:17).

Each of us is well aware that we live in a world of change, a world in which nothing seems to stay the same. About the time we think we have something figured out, it changes and we have to refigure (the compliant teenager, for example, who turned to drugs). Just when we finally have the circumstances of our lives arranged as we want them, somehow the proverbial "rug" gets jerked from under us and everything changes (job loss or marriage problems, for example). The fact of the matter is this: from the moment of conception, each one of us lives in a state of constant flux (change that produces unrest). As we continue to grow and to mature, many of the experiences of life send us very negative messages about change, and, consequently, we develop a very strong resistance to it.

Regardless, however, of personal perception, and even though it sounds like an oxymoron, *change is a part of life that is here to stay!* The good news is that God designed it for our benefit and for His glory. The bad news is that, because of our strong resistance to change, we tend to fight it in order to preserve the status quo, even when the status quo is the very thing that is robbing us of His perfect gift—victorious Christian living.

For reasons that are better left with God, we are very prone to acclimate ourselves to the familiar, even the painfully familiar; consequently, we resist *any* change that might move us out of these familiar places into the not-so-familiar. Sadly, many people (for example, the uneducated, the financially strapped, caretakers, battered women, abused children, victims of affairs) choose to remain in these familiar places, rather than taking the risk of being moved outside their perceived comfort zones, even though their choice is robbing them of God's perfect gift. Fortunately, however, God has what it takes to force a move, and to do so without respect to our preferences, and when He does, it is always good—very good—even though we probably won't agree (at least, not at first).

For example, in my counseling career, I encountered many Christian women who chose to continue living in an abusive relationship because of their fear of being unable to survive alone, their fear of being hurt, their fear of financial loss, or their fear of losing their children to an abusive mate (sometimes all of those). Sadly, they acclimated themselves to the familiar abuse, rather than choosing to break free. Obviously, they were not living victoriously.

Providentially, in all of this change that goes on in and around our lives, change that often precipitates confusion, fear, insecurity, doubt, helplessness, and hopelessness, there is One who never changes. "I, the Lord, do not change" (Malachi 3:6). "Jesus Christ is the same yesterday and today, yes and forever" (Hebrews 13:8). "Every good thing bestowed and every perfect gift is from above, coming down from the Father of lights, with whom there is **no variation, or shifting shadow**" (James 1:17; emphasis, mine).

Somehow, it is very comforting for me to know that, in this great and ever-changing sea we call life, there is someone who never changes, regardless of the circumstances. There is someone in whom there is no variation or shifting shadow, regardless of the degree of the darkness of the moment. And, I might add, there is someone who is the same yesterday, today, and forever. Without Him, I would wander aimlessly through this life, having no sense of direction or purpose; always resisting the very thing I need most—the change that would facilitate my receiving His perfect and timely gift.

Furthermore, in this world of constant change, I am extremely thankful that His Word never changes. "Forever, O Lord, Thy Word is settled in heaven (Psalm 119:89). All flesh is like grass, and all its glory like the flower of grass. The grass withers, and the flower falls off, but the Word of the Lord abides forever" (1 Peter 1:24). For me, there is an incredible peace that comes as the result of my sincere belief that God's Word is sure, steadfast, and eternal. If God said it, that settles it—period.

Why is this so important? It is because it enables us to trust Him, to trust whatever He has said in His Word, without having to worry that He might have changed his mind or that the statute of limitations has run out. For example, you might find yourself in a situation of change that is scaring the wits out of you (you have lost your job and have no hopes of finding one in time to save your house and care for your family), but you still have enough of your wits to turn to the never-changing Word of God. When you do, you find yourself reading this: "For this reason I say to you, do not be anxious for your life, as to what you shall eat; or for your body, as to what you shall put on. For life is more than food, and the body more than clothing. Consider the ravens, for they neither sow nor reap; and they have neither storeroom nor barn; and yet God feeds them; how much more valuable you are than the birds" (Luke 12:22–24)! Wow!

The fact is He sets the course of our lives according to His good pleasure and for His great glory and asks us simply to trust Him and His finished work to get us Home before dark—victorious Christian living, indeed! What an incredibly perfect gift from the Father of Lights, in whom there is no variation or shifting shadow!

6

The Exercise of His Will

> "In the exercise of His will He brought us forth by the word of truth, so that we might be, as it were, the first fruits among His creatures" (James 1:18).

As each of us knows, this subject—the will of God—has been debated and discussed since man learned that he could. Most Christians, however, still do not know what they believe, and the few who think they know have a difficult time defending their beliefs. The evidence is obvious and overwhelming.

In the first place, there are Christians who, although they confess that God is sovereign and, therefore, acts sovereignly, believe that He is, somehow, double-minded, having both a *permissive* will and a *perfect* will. According to this belief system, He allows things to happen that are not a part of His perfect will but well within the parameters of His permissive will. For example, children starve and die in Ethiopia as the result of His permissive will, not His perfect will. In the same way, Christians divorce as the result of His permissive will, not as the result of His perfect will. In either case, according to this mind-set, God has a #1 will and a #2 will—the former, perfect; the latter, obviously, not-so-perfect (at least in our minds).

Furthermore, there are Christians who, although they confess that God is sovereign and, thus, He acts sovereignly, believe that man has a free will and can, therefore, act independently of God's sovereign will. The best examples I know of this are seen in those who believe that God sovereignly wills that every person be saved; however, man can overrule God's sovereign will and choose to reject His offer of salvation; and in those who believe that Jesus shed His blood for everyone; however, it is possible for some to die without experiencing justification by choosing to reject the efficacy of His blood.

Interestingly, according to this mind-set, the efficacy of both God's will and the blood of Jesus are determined by man's choice. In other words, God becomes the victim of man's choice, and man becomes God.

Our text presents us with truth, truth that nullifies each of the above positions: *In the exercise of His will He brought us forth!* There is nothing in this text that would lead one to believe that God has both a permissive will and a perfect will, nor is there anything in this text that would lead one to believe that man has the ability (by using his free will) to act independently of God's will. Much to the contrary, in this text God is seen sovereignly exercising His will and, thereby, bringing us forth from death into life.

If you will notice, this text does not indicate that God exercises His will to "bring us forth" and then makes us the offer to accept or reject the gift. The text clearly tells us that in the exercise of His will He brought us forth from death to life—period! In other words, He gave life to the dead. Surely it is obvious that the dead cannot possibly do anything, anything at all. This fact, in and of itself, makes it very necessary that God's will always prevails, as the dead have no will, none whatsoever.

We should be very thankful that He chose to take full responsibility for our redemption; otherwise, we would all be eternally lost. If we were not so fleshly and so self-absorbed, we would be rejoicing that even one sinner is saved, regardless of who that one might be!

Just for the record, these are facts about our text: The phrase *in the exercise of His will* translates the aorist passive participle of the verb βουλομαι (boo-lo-mi), which expresses the idea of the deliberate and specific exercise of volition. The phrase is also in the emphatic position in the Greek, reinforcing the truth that God's sovereign and uninfluenced will is the source and basis of the new birth.

The fact is the *only* way life can be given to those who are dead is through the sovereign and uninfluenced will of God! Those who are dead to God, the unregenerate, obviously, have *no* desire to turn from sin, and they certainly have no desire for Jesus. In fact, they do not even know that they are dead! They have but one hope, and that hope is providentially linked to God's sovereign and uninfluenced will.

This analogy is probably too simple; however, I offer it. Although millions and millions of children have been born into the world, not one of them has been born as the result of his or her wish. In every instance, conception and birth have been completely outside of his or her consciousness and control. The newborn is merely a passive recipient of the will and action of its parents. In the same way, millions of Christians have been born again into the family of God since its inception; however, not one of them has been born again as the result of his or her wish. We are redeemed, my dear brothers and sisters, as the result of God exercising His will to bring us forth—out of darkness and into His marvelous light!

Now, having said that, allow me to say that after God, in the exercise of His will, brings us forth as the first fruits of His creations, after He brings us forth out of darkness and into His marvelous light, we do have the freedom of will to make choices. However, let me be quick to point out that that freedom of will is confined by the parameters of God's providence. In other words, as a believer you can and will make all kinds of choices—some wise and some unwise—however, you cannot make a choice that overrules the choices He has already made concerning your life. For example, you can choose for lunch to eat a hamburger rather than a salad; however, you cannot choose to lose the gift of eternal life. You can choose to fly to New York rather than taking a bus; however, you cannot choose not to love. Why? Love is a fruit of the Spirit, the Holy Spirit, who lives and loves in you.

You can also choose to live as if you are still under the jurisdiction of the law; however, you cannot choose for the law to be your means to righteousness. Why? Because Jesus is your righteousness, and He lives in you, and that is forever settled in Heaven.

The long and short of it is this: Thank God that He brought you forth according to the exercise of His will; otherwise, you would still be living in darkness, without hope and damned to eternal death.

7

The Word of Truth

"In the exercise of His will He brought us forth by the word of truth, so that we might be, as it were, the first fruits among His creatures" (James 1:18).

To say the least, the events leading up to and including Jesus's crucifixion had been mind-boggling to His followers, especially to those who were closest to Him. Although only a precious few were near the cross at the time of His crucifixion, everyone who loved Him, including those who had distanced themselves, was befuddled and afraid. In the end, at least from their perspective, God's word meant nothing because Jesus was dead. Each of them wondered just who would be next in line for this horrible death. The truth is they had placed all of their hope and trust in Him, and now they felt betrayed and afraid.

Three very long and agonizing days passed as they waited and wondered in fearful anxiety. Over and over they asked, "Why did Jesus build us up only to let us down—way down? If He is who He claims to be, why didn't He save Himself?"

Little did they know about the faithfulness and the power of the Word of Truth!

It was yet dark, very early in the morning on the first day of the week, when Mary Magdalene approached Jesus's tomb and discovered that the stone had been taken away. Her first look inside the opened door served only to exacerbate the fear and anxiety she was already experiencing. Her adrenalin was flowing like never before, her heart was beating so fast that it could barely pump blood, and her feet were racing as fast as she could move them. Even so, she felt frozen in time. It seemed that every moment she had experienced with Jesus over the past several years was flashing before her eyes, leaving her with smothering ambivalence—love and hate; fear and faith; doom and hope! She found Peter and John and told them what she had seen. The look on her face sent them running to the tomb, only to find it empty, just as Mary had told them. Bewildered and confused, they returned home, *but Mary* refused to leave. Something deep within her heart, a force far greater than any she had ever known, simply would not let her leave.

Then it happened just as He had promised: "Destroy this temple, and in three days I will raise it up" (John 2:19)! Immediately, He began speaking to her, asking her these two simple but timely questions, "Woman, why are you weeping? Whom are you seeking?" (John 20:15a). Mary turned and looked directly into His eyes but what she saw was simply too good to be true. She immediately convinced herself that He was merely the gardener. "Sir, if you have carried Him away, please tell me where you have laid Him, and I will take Him away" (John 20:15b), she begged. Jesus could stand it no longer. He loved her too much to prolong her agony! In the exercise of His will and with the Word of Truth expressed in this single exclamation— *Mary!*—He brought her forth out of the darkness and confusion and bewilderment that had controlled her life and placed her into His marvelous light and into the freedom and joy it brings.

Instinctively, she fell into His loving, warm embrace. Listen to her first verbal response: *I have seen the Lord!*

This Word of Truth to which James refers is the same power that God used to create the universe and everything it contains. It is the very same power that God used to bring forth Jesus out of His "borrowed" tomb. It is the same power that enables the delicate lily to push through the stubborn sod. It is the power that brought forth Lazarus from his grave. It is the power that Jesus used to heal the leper and give sight to the blind.

It appears that many believers live as if Jesus is some weak, impotent shell of man, who is hiding somewhere in the shadows, fearing for His life. The scriptures simply do not confirm that belief system. When the Word of Truth speaks, whatever He says is—period. And I might add this: He is ever speaking to His Father in your behalf!

8

Quick to Hear

> "This you know, my beloved brethren. But let everyone be quick to hear, slow to speak, and slow to anger; for the anger of man does not achieve the righteousness of God" (James 1:19–20).

In this text, James is giving us three directives that we all find hard to follow—be quick to hear; be slow to speak, and be slow to anger. The truth is few of us (probably none of us!) can lay claim to having mastered even one of these, much less all three of them. In light of that fact, it will probably behoove us to take a careful look at each of these.

After almost thirty-three years as a pastor and counselor, it has become very obvious to me that very few people actually listen at all. Listening is certainly not something we are quick to do. In order to have integrity with you, I will have to place myself in that category. Listening simply does not come easy. The fact is it takes Holy Spirit-led practice and lots of it.

I am certain that you can quickly recall an experience, probably a very recent one, where you were attempting to tell someone something that was very important to you, but early

on you realized that they were not listening. If fact, if you had been brave enough to ask him what you had just told him, he would have been hard put to tell you.

You can also recall an example where you were telling someone something that was very important to you, e.g., you just bought a new car, only to have her interrupt you to tell you about the car she bought the week before. In other words, she turned the focus off of you and onto her.

If you will be honest, you will have to admit that you are guilty of the same thing. While someone was talking to you, instead of listening, you were rehearsing in your mind how you would tell your story. Of course, in your mind your story is a bit better than his story, so you are convinced that he will enjoy it. A wrong assumption! Instead of joy, he will feel rejection.

Many years ago, I read a booklet entitled "The Awesome Power of the Listening Ear." It was so long ago that I no longer remember the author's name, but I do remember much of what he had to say. To say the least, it profoundly affected my life, especially my desire to become a good listener. The fact is everyone likes a good listener and few (if any) enjoy being around someone who has "ratchet jaw" (talks all the time)!

The most powerful people in my life and in your life are those who are quick to listen, those who make it their business to focus on hearing what others are saying. These people are powerful because we respect them and feel comfortable in their presence. We truly believe that they are interested in our lives, that they have, somehow, managed to put into practice these words of the Apostle Paul: "Do nothing from selfishness or empty conceit, but with humility of mind let each of you regard one another as more important than himself; do not merely look out for your own personal interests, but also for the interests of others" (Philippians 2:3–4).

9

Slow to Speak

"This you know, my beloved brethren. But let everyone be quick to hear, slow to speak, and slow to anger; for the anger of man does not achieve the righteousness of God" (James 1:19–20).

Every believer that I have ever known could profit from giving some thought to this part of our text—slow to speak. Yes, I know that there are some people who never seem to say anything because they are afraid and intimidated, and that is sad. They seem to live in a cocoon of emotional insulation that keeps them inside and, thus, protected from those on the outside. However, I also know some people who speak very little, not out of fear but out of caution, wanting to be certain that what they are about to say is really worth saying. I can only assume that they have read these words: *But avoid worldly and empty chatter, for it will lead to further ungodliness, and their talk will spread like gangrene* (2 Timothy 16–17). In my opinion, these are the people to whom James is referring.

I am certain that you can recall a recent example of when you were much too quick to speak and, as a result, spent quite a bit of time regretting what you said. This one comes to my mind, even as I write these words: I had set aside a day to write, trying to finish this book and get it to the publisher. I was busy doing just that, when my wife called to me, from her perch on the sofa with her cup of coffee and the newspaper, asking me to take the exterminator down to the basement to show him where to spray. In a flash, I got out of my computer chair and, walking toward her, said, "Yes, but I have told you that I have dedicated this time to write, and every time you call me you distract me, and I lose my thought process. I guess I can leave my office here at home and go to the church office!" As soon as the words came out of my mouth, I regretted saying them, not because they were not true, but because they hurt her. Yes, I did apologize.

Do I think God is now angry with me because I was quick to speak? No! Do I think He would have thought more of me, had I not been so quick to speak? No! Do I think I hurt God's feelings because I was so quick to speak? No, definitely not! My relationship with God is settled forever, as the result of Jesus's finished work. Do I think my wife was angry? Yes! Do I think she thinks less of me because I was so quick to speak? No, but I do think I hurt her feelings, which is why being so quick to speak is not a good thing.

You already know this, but words spoken are very difficult to retract, and, I might add, words spoken too quickly are usually impossible to retract. The sad truth is this: most people never remember the good things we say, but they never forget the hurtful things we say, especially when they are spoken too quickly, which they usually are.

10

Slow to Anger

"This you know, my beloved brethren. But let everyone be quick to hear, slow to speak, and slow to anger; for the anger of man does not achieve the righteousness of God" (James 1:19–20).

Thankfully, this verse does not exclude our being angry; instead, it warns us to be slow about becoming angry. However, even with this concession, from what I have been able to observe, anger management is no small accomplishment. Most of the Christians who are alive today ignored the "go slow" warning sign long ago and, consequently, anger has become the "normal" way of the Christian life. In order for someone to think he needs a course in anger management, things have to get bad—really bad!

As you know, most of us do quite well at expressing anger; albeit, some tend to be more covert than others—passive aggression (sitting down on the outside but standing up on the inside) as opposed to active aggression (standing up on the outside and the inside). Even so, those we target become victims of our abusive behavior, and, strangely, they are most often those we love most.

Let me hasten to remind you that anger, in and of itself, is not evil or sinful, as is evidenced by the fact that Jesus Himself acted angrily. "And he said to them, 'Is it lawful on the Sabbath to do good or to do harm, to save a life or to kill?' But they kept silent. **And after looking around at them with anger,** grieved at their hardness of heart, He said to the man, 'Stretch out your hand.' And he stretched it out, and his hand was restored" (Mark 3:4–5; emphasis mine). Of course, we all know about the anger He exhibited with the moneychangers in the temple (see Matthew 21:12–13). Furthermore, God exhibited anger on many occasions (see Hebrews 3:10, for an example).

Paul emphasized this with these words: "Be angry, and do not sin; do not let the sun go down on your anger, and do not give the devil an opportunity" (Ephesians 4:26–27). In other words, it is completely within the parameters of righteousness for us to exhibit anger; however, when we do, we must do so without sinning because we do not want to give the devil an opportunity to deceive us.

Obviously, one of the keys to success lies within how quickly we forgive (release our anger) those with whom we are angry. As each of us knows that stored anger is *not* a good thing because it breeds the unquenchable desire to "get even" with the "enemy" who hurt us. Unfortunately, that desire manifests itself in very hurtful and damaging ways, especially in light of the fact that we most often target our anger at those we love most, rather than the one(s) who hurt us.

This is tragic but, nevertheless, true: we become slaves of the one who hurt us *unless* we are quick to forgive, (i.e., quick to cancel the debt he created when he hurt us). In my opinion, the last person we should want to be enslaved to is the person who hurt us. You see, forgiveness is not for the one who hurt us, but for us, specifically you, if you were hurt. How quick are you to forgive? Are you presently holding a grudge? If you are, then you are someone's slave, namely the person who hurt you. Let the anger go through forgiveness, and you will be free!

Having said that, let me remind you of this: in the heat of the battle, most of us completely forget that our real enemy is Satan, not the one who hurt us. As a result, we seldom ever know what it means to be "more than conquerors" when it comes to anger management. Thankfully, Paul has given us the truth and the key to overcoming sinful anger: "For our struggle is not against flesh and blood, but against the rulers, against the powers, against the world forces of this darkness, against the spiritual forces of wickedness in the heavenly places" (Ephesians 6:12). May we never forget it!

Now, back to the text in which we are warned to do three things, each of which carries requirements that we do not meet very readily: (1) be quick to hear, which requires *attentive listening*; (2) be slow to speak, which requires *incredible patience*; and (3) be slow to anger, which requires *relentless forgiveness*.

In the end, it becomes quite obvious that we desperately need a Savior, One who has been tempted in every way that we are tempted, including not to listen, not to be patient, and, not to forgive. Wow! We have One in Jesus! I am so glad (thankful) that, even though He was tempted in every way that we are tempted, He *never* yielded to the pressure and, therefore, never gave Satan an opportunity.

In light of our text, I want to encourage each of us to run to Him and cast ourselves upon Him because He really does care for us. This is the secret: Christ in you, your hope of glory, even when it comes to anger management!

11
Humbly Receiving the Implanted Word

"Therefore putting aside all filthiness and all that remains of wickedness, in humility receive the word implanted, which is able to save your souls" (James 1:21).

There is probably nothing more deserving of the believer's attention than James's encouraging us to receive the implanted word, unless it is his admonition for us *to receive it humbly*, having put aside all filthiness and wickedness. Surely, we should give this passage our undivided attention.

First, James appears to be following his usual "legalistic" approach to Christianity when he places the criteria of our putting aside all filthiness and our putting aside all that remains of wickedness, before we can "humbly" receive the implanted word. Obviously, each of us knows (and so did James) that we will never achieve this goal, unless someone comes to our rescue, and this "someone" must be the One who has a perfect record before the eternal God, namely, Jesus. If each of us would be honest, we would have to admit that without the benefit of His finished work, this verse would be very discouraging.

Second, humility is not something we achieve as the result of our self-righteous attempts at laying aside all filthiness and all that remains of wickedness; instead, it is the gift God gives to us when we finally realize our dependence upon Him for everything, especially for our victory over sin. It is the gift He bestows upon us when we finally begin to rest in Jesus's finished work. If, through our own strength, we could lay aside all filthiness and wickedness and, thereby, achieve humility, we would have to change its definition. Achieved humility is an oxymoron!

Third, we cannot, however, diminish the importance of our *putting aside all filthiness and all that remains of wickedness*, and we cannot because humility, the apparent prerequisite for our receiving the implanted word, is the fruit of our having done so. The question with which we must grapple is this: what is the key to our allowing Jesus to end our relationship with filthiness and wickedness and, thereby, to produce the fruit of humility in our lives? The answer, of course, lies in whether we believe the true gospel. The fact is any other gospel (which is really no gospel) always leads to self-righteous independence and completely obscures the significance of Jesus's vicarious and finished work.

A gospel that makes you the centerpiece will never set you free from the filthiness and wickedness to which James refers. The true gospel, the one that makes Jesus the centerpiece, always and forever sets you free from both. Read carefully what Paul had to say about these "other" gospels: "But even though we, or an angel from heaven, should preach to you a gospel contrary to that which we have preached to you, let him be accursed. As we have said before, so I say again now, if any man is preaching to you a gospel contrary to that which you have received, let him be accursed" (Galatians 1:8–9).

Fourth, the implanted word, to which James refers, is the imperishable seed of the word of God that He implanted within us and by which we were born again of the Spirit of God.

It is important to note James's use of the word *receive,* as it distinguishes God's implanting the word within us and our receiving it. In other words, there is a significant difference between our having been given a gift and in our receiving the gift. For example, many fathers have given their daughters in marriage, but that does not mean the husband actually received the gift. To be sure, the gift was given, but was it received? I might add this: humility *is* the perquisite! Husbands never receive their wives (and vice versa) until and unless they have laid aside the enemies of humility—filthiness and wickedness. Every believer has been given the imperishable seed of the word of God; however, few believers really receive the word of God because doing so carries the prerequisite of humility, and humility requires absolute dependence upon the finished work of Jesus. In other words, humility breeds trust in the implanted word!

Fifth, James tells us that when this implanted word is received, it is able to save our souls.[3] Notice his use of the word *soul* here, as opposed to *spirit.* To be sure, the imperishable seed of the word of God does, indeed, give us life and, thereby, save us from sin and death; however, when it is *received* it also saves our souls—mind, will, and emotions. The implanted word, received, changes the way we think, what we desire, and how we feel. It opens the door for us to begin to think with the mind of Christ, to desire the things of the Spirit, and to feel compassion, rather than bitterness.

Make no mistake, however, regarding the efficacy of the implanted Word concerning salvation (justification, sanctification, and glorification). Its effectiveness to produce salvation is dependent upon nothing, not even our receiving it. The efficacy of the implanted Word is in the Word itself.

---

3 For our discussion here, "spirit" refers to that part of man that relates directly with God; whereas, "soul" refers to the mind (that with which we think), the will (that with which we make decisions), and the emotions (that with which we feel).

Finally, maybe Paul said it best after all: "But you did not learn Christ in this way, if indeed you have heard Him and have been taught in Him, just as truth is in Jesus, that, in reference to your former manner of life, you lay aside the old self, which is being corrupted in accordance with the lusts of deceit, and that you be renewed in the spirit of your mind, and put on the new self, which in the likeness of God has been created in righteousness and holiness of the truth" (Ephesians 4:20–24).

12
Obeying the Word

> "But prove yourselves doers of the word, and not merely hearers who delude themselves. For if anyone is a hearer of the word and not a doer, he is like a man who looks at his natural face in a mirror; for once he has looked at himself and gone away, he has immediately forgotten what kind of person he was. But one who looks intently at the perfect law, the law of liberty, and abides by it, not having become a forgetful hearer but an effectual doer, this man shall be blessed in what he does" (James 1:22–25).

Caution! Please do not make the same mistake that most make when they read this passage. At first glance, it might appear that James, once again, is being a legalist; however, Christianity has nothing to do with legalism. The two are on opposite ends of the theological spectrum. Christianity, on the one hand, is about an intimate love affair with Jesus, one that He not only conceived, but also nurtures, and guarantees. Legalism, on the other hand, is about a self-righteous love affair with one's self and, therefore, not Christianity at all. Having said that, let us take a closer look at this text.

The "word" to which James refers in this text is the very same "word" to which he referred in the previous passage—the pure, unadulterated word of God, the word by which we were born again, the word that became flesh and dwelt among us, the word that is not only able to save us from the guilt, power, and judgment of sin, but also is able to save our souls.

As you can see, James is encouraging us not to be mere hearers of this word, but to be doers of it. He is preparing us for what he will tell us in the next chapter: "Even so faith, if it has no works, is dead, being by itself" (James 2:17). Regardless of how one might interpret this passage, the fact is most believers have heard far more than they are doing! It does not take a "rocket scientist" to realize that most churchgoers are very content being mere recipients of the preached word—"I really enjoyed that sermon!" This "contentment" is short-lived, however, if someone even hints at putting the preached word into action. In my opinion, there is good reason for this.

Take, for example, the person who, having read James's directive, listens with interest to the Sunday sermon entitled "Love Your Enemies" and eagerly responds to the preacher's invitation to become a doer of this "preached word." How long does it take before he becomes discouraged—very discouraged? It doesn't take very long because he simply cannot love his enemies.

Change the scenario and let the sermon topic be this: "Will a Man Rob God?" Our eager man now determines to be a doer of this "preached word," but it doesn't take long before he begins to feel that he is robbing God because (from his perspective) he cannot tithe and continue to pay his bills. To be sure, he wants to tithe and, thereby, to be a faithful doer of this word; however, he fails over and over again. Why? Is it not obvious? He simply cannot be obedient. Sadly, many of those who do give the proverbial 10 percent of their income to their local church honestly believe they are being obedient and are, thus, gaining favor with God. Deception, indeed! Interestingly, many of those who give that "10 percent" do so at the expense of paying their bills, and thus rob their creditors.

To be sure, the Bible's list is not short when it comes to commandments, principles, and directives; however, when it comes to our reaching God's standard regarding these commandments and principles and directives, we always come up short—very short! We do, however, have James's passage, and we must deal with it for what it is—the Word of God.

Notice James's reminder that those who "hear" without "doing" delude (deceive) themselves! In my opinion, this is a significant key to our understanding this passage. You see, those who fall into the aforementioned category, those who purpose to be obedient but continue to fail, who, nevertheless, believe their "almost" is good enough, have, indeed, deceived themselves! They diligently continue trying to be doers of the word, sincerely believing that, because God understands their weaknesses and limitations, He will, therefore, excuse their failures. After all, He is the God of Love! To be sure, these have not only deceived themselves, but also find themselves having to live with the fruit of this deception—fatigue, frustration, and burnout, not to mention, hypocrisy (they, obviously, must pretend that they are obedient).

Interestingly, James compares this person, who is a hearer of the word but not a doer of the word, with the man who looks (intensely gazes, literally) at his face in a mirror and then walks away, forgetting (doing nothing about) everything he just witnessed. In other words, the person who hears the word but never becomes a doer of the word is guilty of the same thing. He hears and then walks away forgetting (doing nothing about) everything he just heard. This man has, indeed, deceived himself because he believes his "hearing" is, somehow, sufficient to gain God's approval and acceptance. In other words, being a "doer of the word" is unnecessary. He is what I would label an antinomian—one without law.

Now, notice what James accomplishes as he *contrasts* the person who is a hearer of the word but not a doer of the word, with the person who looks intently at the perfect law, the law of liberty, and abides by it, not having become a forgetful hearer but an effectual doer. Masterfully, he shifts the focus from the Law of Moses (the law of sin and death) onto the Law of the Spirit of Life in Christ Jesus (the perfect law; the law of liberty).

Think with me. The Law of Moses is an imperfect law because it cannot impart freedom, and it cannot because we cannot abide by it (God intentionally set the standard—perfection—too high in order to drive us to Jesus); whereas, the Law of the Spirit of Life in Christ Jesus is the perfect law because it is the law by which God places us into Christ Jesus and, thereby, declares us righteous (fully meeting God's standard), having set us free from sin's guilt, power, and judgment!

Having established this, it is much easier to see James's heart as he wrote about our being doers of the word and not mere hearers. You see, our being a doer of the word is *not* in any way related to our self-righteous efforts to keep the commandments (*thou shalt have no other gods before Me*) or to follow various biblical principles (*it is better to give than to receive*) or to obey various directives (*love your enemies*). Instead, it has all to do with our resting in His finished work and, thereby, walking in the works—the good works—that He prepared for us from the foundation of the world, that we might walk in them (see Ephesians 2:10). In other words, the success of our being doers of the word does not depend upon our continued works but upon His finished work.

In summary, if I am going to be a doer of the word and not merely a hearer, I must learn to trust the work He finished in my behalf. I must cease striving to do something significant enough to earn His approval and acceptance, and, merely, rest in the fact that Jesus accomplished that work for me through His vicarious death and resurrection. To do otherwise, is to deceive myself into believing that His finished work is inadequate and, therefore, needs my "finishing touches," and that is, indeed, deception.

In the end, the person who is "doing" the word of God is the person who is trusting in the finished work of Jesus, not in his own self-righteous efforts to justify himself. This person, rather than wasting his life striving to meet the expectations of others, rather than selling his soul to some employer an hour at the time, is free to enjoy his life pursuing his passion! What the Holy Spirit accomplishes through this person is quite amazing! "And I heard a voice from Heaven, saying, 'Write, Blessed are the dead who die in the Lord from now on!' 'Yes,' says the Spirit, 'that they may rest from their labors, for their deeds follow with them'" (Revelation 14:13).

13

The Tongue: A Restless Evil and Full of Deadly Poison

> "If anyone thinks himself to be religious, and yet does not bridle the tongue but deceives his own heart, this man's religion is worthless. This is pure and undefiled religion in the sight of our God and Father, to visit orphans and widows in their distress, and to keep oneself unstained by the world" (James 1:26–27).

Interestingly, the Greek word in verse 26, which is translated *religious,* is the word θρησκοσ (threskos), which refers to the external aspects of divine service—the washings, the cleansings, the sacrifices, the traditions, the ceremonial laws, as well as the Law of Moses. As you know, for the Jew the externals of divine service were not only demanding but also overwhelming. You can rest assured that they kept every serious Jew busy—very busy. Can you imagine, for example, trying to obey the 210 external requirements for keeping the Sabbath holy? Remember this: in their minds, their standing not only within the Jewish community and its leadership, but also with God was determined by how well they maintained the externals—the religious services—of Judaism.

With that in mind, you can imagine how the typical struggling Jew, not to mention those who believed that they were measuring up to the standard of holiness, especially the Pharisees, responded to this passage. According to James, when it comes to the externals of the Jewish faith, one could pass every test but fail to bridle his tongue and, consequently, fail the entire test. If this were the standard used today to differentiate between non-Christians and Christians, there would be no Christians because not one of us can tame his tongue! Actually, James is very clear in his assessment; this man's religion is worthless! To be sure, all religion is worthless because it is always tied to the externals—man's performance—rather than to the internals—Jesus's vicarious performance.

If you will wind the film forward a bit, you will discover that James makes several more difficult (actually, very difficult) comments about the tongue, comments that substantiate the worthlessness of religion: "If anyone does not stumble in what he says (Who, pray tell would that be?), he is a perfect man, able to bridle the whole body as well. Behold how great a fire is set aflame by such a small flame. And *the tongue is a fire*, the very world of iniquity; *the tongue is set among our members as that which defiles the entire body, and sets on fire the course of our life (our existence)*, and is *set on fire by hell*. For every species of beasts and birds, of reptiles and creatures of the sea, is tamed, and has been tamed by the human race. But *no one can tame the tongue; it is a restless evil and full of deadly poison*. With it we bless our Lord and Father; and with it we curse men, who have been made in the likeness of God; from the same mouth come both blessing and cursing. My brethren, these things ought not to be this way" (selected from James 2; emphasis and parenthetical comment, mine).

With this in mind, it is certainly safe to conclude that all religion is worthless because, obviously, no one can tame the tongue. It is a fire that is set on fire by hell and, consequently, sets on fire the course of our lives, thereby defiling the entire body. The tongue is a restless evil and full of deadly poison, even the tongues of James and Mother Teresa!

Interestingly, in light of all the negative things that James says about the tongue, in spite of the sense of hopelessness that his message brings, he does bring into his message this ray of hope: "My brethren, these things ought not to be this way" (James 3:10b). In other words, there is a way out, there is another option, there is a road to victory, and there is a way to overcome! What, pray tell is it?

In the next verse of our text (verse 27), James informs us that the other option lies in our being identified not with the externals of religious worship but with that which, in the sight of God, is pure and undefiled religion, namely, visiting orphans and widows in their distress (relationships with others within the body of Christ), and keeping ourselves unstained by the world (relationship with God)! James is now making a clear distinction between "impure and defiled religion" (traditional Judaism) and "pure and undefiled religion" (true Christianity). Notice how ingeniously he accomplishes this, as he moves us from obedience to the external trappings of traditional Judaism, to the internal motivations of both the horizontal (visit orphans and widows in their distress) and the vertical (keep yourself unstained by the world) relationships of Christianity.

You see, in this arena, the tongue is no longer the issue of righteousness, and bridling the tongue (externals) is no longer the requirement for holiness in worship; instead, the issue is relationships (horizontal and vertical) and the requirement is the humility of faith in Jesus. As evidence, notice the next verse: "My brethren, do not hold your faith in our glorious Lord Jesus Christ with an attitude of personal favoritism" (James 2:1). In this verse, James clearly links the vertical relationships (our relationship with the Father, Son, and Holy Spirit) and the horizontal relationships (our relationships with one another within the Body of Christ) with the humility of faith. This faith, I might add, is the very same faith that God used to reckon Abraham as a righteous man, the faith that gave him permanent and bold access into the Holy of Holies, in spite of the fact that he could not tame his tongue.

You see, James knew a secret that the religious world will never know because they are self-centered and self-focused, and, therefore, too busy trying to look, act, and feel religious. The secret is this: when one's relationship with the Father, Son, and Holy Spirit (the vertical) and his relationship with others within the Body of Christ (the horizontal) becomes paramount in his heart, something happens to his tongue. "For the mouth speaks out of that which fills the heart" (Matthew 12:34). To be sure, the mouth speaks out of the abundance of the heart!

In conclusion, our being religious—our futile attempts at practicing the externals, especially our attempts at taming the tongue—is always worthless before God, and it is because it can only breed self-righteousness, which God hates. However, pure and undefiled religion—the result of the finished work of Jesus in our behalf, the work that makes relationship with Him and with others paramount in our hearts—is always highly treasured before God, and it is because it produces the righteousness of Christ, which God loves. In the end, the fruit of righteousness—loving relationships with Him and with others—fills the heart, and out of that heart, the mouth lovingly speaks truth. Maybe this is a bit of what Ezekiel had in mind when he wrote these words: "Moreover, I will give you a new heart and put a new spirit within you; and I will remove the heart of stone from your flesh and give you a heart of flesh. And I will put My Spirit within you and cause you to walk in My statutes, and you will be careful to observe My ordinances" (Ezekiel 36:26–27).

14

Partiality: Judging with Evil Motives

> "My brethren, do not hold your faith in our glorious Lord Jesus Christ with an attitude of personal favoritism. For if a man comes into your assembly with a gold ring and dressed in fine clothes, and there also comes in a poor man in dirty clothes, and you pay special attention to the one who is wearing the fine clothes, and say, 'You sit here in a good place,' and you say to the poor man, 'You stand over there, or sit down by my footstool,' have you not made distinctions among yourselves, and become judges with evil motives?" (James 2:1–4).

It was a beautiful Sunday morning, and the church was packed with worshippers, all of whom were dressed in their Sunday finest. It was no secret in this place that "gold rings and fine clothes" were equated with righteousness—the finer the gold and clothes, the finer the righteousness. The pastor, himself, was dressed to the hilt—Hickey Freeman suit, alligator shoes, starched shirt, silk tie, gold ring, et al. The choir members were decked out in beautiful robes, and a huge arrangement of fresh flowers graced the chancel. The stage was set for worship—grand and glorious worship!

A few minutes into this magnificent service, in walked a dirty, smelly street person, who was dressed in a long black coat that bore the stench of stale beer and cigarette smoke. His mismatched shoes were tattered, dirty, dog-eared sneakers he probably found abandoned along the highway. He wore a ring, to be sure; however, it was made of the aluminum foil from a chewing gum wrapper. His hair was nasty and matted, yet it stood out in all directions. Interestingly, he boldly entered the sanctuary through one of the side doors near the chancel and took his seat on the first pew—front and center.

Although everyone who was seated anywhere near the front saw this man when he entered, it took the pastor a while to realize his presence. Ironically, he was in the middle of his weekly *appeal for evangelism*, when he saw him. He was fervently encouraging the congregation to go out into the highways and hedges and invite the lost to this church, when their eyes met. His reaction was one of horror! He quickly finished his appeal, returned to his seat, and picked up the phone he used to communicate with the sound technicians, the ushers, and the security officers. In less than a minute, two security officers were removing this "vermin" from the sanctuary! All in all, his worship experience lasted less than three minutes, and he was back on the street, having been warned never to return.

Just for the record: I actually witnessed this experience "up close and personal" because this "vermin" sat in close proximity to me. Yes, I have "doctored" some of the details— Hickey Freeman suits, gold rings, silk ties, and alligator shoes— however, this event actually took place in a Protestant church, a church that, from all outward appearances, truly desired to be involved in evangelism.

In their exuberance to be evangelistic, the leadership overlooked this important detail: Jesus came not to reach people who are like Him—holy, righteous, and accepted by God—but to reach the "vermin" of the world—the filthy, smelly, wine-bibbing, gluttonous sinners! Unfortunately, when this church talked about evangelism, about inviting the lost to church, what it really meant was this: invite people who are like us—educated, middle to upper class, blue and/or white collar, freshly perfumed, well-dressed, respectable citizens—not the "vermin" of the world. We certainly do *not* want to have our family members, especially our children, associate with or be influenced by such worthless scum! Surely there are plenty of our "kind" that we can reach, without having to include the "vermin" of the world.

I must tell you that, ever since the Sunday this man was escorted out of the sanctuary, I have wondered if he might not have been Jesus. To be sure, he acted like Him! I think he even looked like Him! He never put up a fight nor did he speak an unkind word; instead, he willingly and quietly walked up the aisle and out the door, while most probably muttered, "A winebibber and a glutton! How dare he interrupt our glorious, Christ-centered worship service?"

Now back to our text: *Do not hold your faith in our glorious Lord Jesus Christ with an attitude of personal favoritism.* Can you see it? Personal favoritism is not only a symptom of self-centeredness, but also a symptom of pride and arrogance. It not only declares (and clearly so) one's lack of understanding concerning the significance of his/her own sinfulness, but also his/her propensity toward judging others with evil motives.

"Listen, my beloved brethren: did not God choose the poor of this world to be rich in faith and heirs of the kingdom which He promised to those who love Him? But you have dishonored the poor man. Is it not the rich who oppress you and personally drag you into court? Do they not blaspheme the fair name by which you have been called?" (James 2:5–7).

Maybe, just maybe, each of us should be reminded of our Adamic roots: "What then: Are we better than they? Not at all; for we have already charged that both Jews and Greeks are all under sin; as it is written, 'There is none righteous, not even one; there is none who understands, there is none who seeks for God; All have turned aside, together they have become useless; There is none who does good, there is not even one. Their throat is an open grave, with their tongues they keep deceiving, the poison of asps is under their lips; whose mouth is full of cursing and bitterness; their feet are swift to shed blood. Destruction and misery are in their paths, and the path of peace have they not known. There is no fear of God before their eyes'" (Romans 3:9–18).

In light of this, I find these words of Paul quite incredible: "For while we were still helpless, at the right time Christ died for the ungodly. For one will hardly die for a righteous man; though perhaps for the good man someone would dare even to die. But God demonstrates his own love toward us, in that while we were yet sinners, Christ died for us" (Romans 5:6–8).

You see, when that "vermin" entered the sanctuary on that beautiful Sunday morning, I have the strong feeling that it was Jesus, dressed as one who came to reach "vermin"; however, most of the congregation, holding their faith in Jesus with an attitude of personal favoritism, never saw themselves as such and, consequently, missed Him and His offer completely. I will always wonder if that day did not change the course of the life of that church. To be sure, by its behavior, it clearly announced its mission and purpose, which from what I can see does not differ from the mission and purpose of most churches! In our self-centered, self-righteous piousness, we dishonor the "poor man" without even realizing it, and in so doing, with evil motives, we judge and condemn others, not to mention ourselves.

15

Mercy Triumphs over Judgment

"If, however, you are fulfilling the royal law, according to the Scripture, 'You shall love your neighbor as yourself,' you are doing well. But if you show partiality, you are committing sin and are convicted by the Law as transgressors. For whoever keeps the whole law and yet stumbles in one point, he has become guilty of all. For He who said, 'Do not commit adultery,' also said, 'Do not commit murder.' Now if you do not commit adultery, but do commit murder, you have become a transgressor of the Law. So speak and so act, as those who are to be judged by the law of liberty. For judgment will be merciless to one who has shown no mercy; mercy triumphs over judgment" (James 2:8–13).

In the first seven verses of this chapter, James makes it clear that the common practice of showing favoritism toward those who have more seemliness—the ones with *fine clothes and gold rings*—is unacceptable, because, in doing so, we become judges with evil motives. He goes on to show us how foolish it is to honor the one who will oppress us and drag us into court, even blaspheme the fair name by which we have been called, while dishonoring the one who will respond to us with love and compassion, especially in light of the fact that God chose the poor of this world to be rich in faith and heirs of the kingdom that He promised to those who love Him.

In verse 8, however, he begins to show us God's way of relating to others—loving our neighbors as we love ourselves and, thus, fulfilling the royal law. On the one hand, when we show favoritism and, thereby, become judges with evil motives, the law convicts us as transgressors, and we become guilty of the entire law; however, on the other hand, when we love others as we love ourselves and, thereby, fulfill the royal law, we do well.

In my journey, I have met many people who sincerely believe that they are very good at keeping God's Law. In fact, I met one preacher who actually told me that he perfectly kept God's Law. What this preacher failed to see was that he was a very judgmental in his preaching. Pharisees are the "law-keepers" and they are, consequently, always judgmental. It was obvious that the mission of this preacher's messages was not only to cause his members to feel a consciousness of their sins, but also to cause them to feel the guilt of their sins. I am sure that he loved this particular text, as it gave him much fodder for his legalistic messages.

Jesus made it clear that the entire law is summed up in "love your neighbor as yourself"(see Galatians 5:14); however, the modern-day Pharisees, those who think they are doing such a good job of keeping the law, of obeying God, somehow fail to realize that their judgmental attitudes project anything but love.

Having said that, in the next chapter I want to raise these questions:

1. What is the royal law?
2. How can loving others as we love ourselves be a good thing, especially in light of the fact that most (if not all) of us love ourselves so selfishly?
3. How can we reconcile the fact that God has forgiven us for all of our sins and declared us to be as righteous as Jesus is righteous, with James's

declaration that the law convicts us as transgressors of the entire law, when we show partiality?

Before you turn to the next chapter, please give some careful thought to the message your life is sending to those in your "world." Would they label you as "judgmental"? Be courageous enough to ask a few of them.

16

What Is the Royal Law?

"If, however, you are fulfilling the royal law, according to the Scripture, 'You shall love your neighbor as yourself,' you are doing well. But if you show partiality, you are committing sin and are convicted by the Law as transgressors. For whoever keeps the whole law and yet stumbles in one point, he has become guilty of all. For He who said, 'Do not commit adultery,' also said, 'Do not commit murder.' Now if you do not commit adultery, but do commit murder, you have become a transgressor of the Law. So speak and so act, as those who are to be judged by the law of liberty. For judgment will be merciless to one who has shown no mercy; mercy triumphs over judgment" (James 2:8–13).

The royal law is, obviously, the Law of our King—Jesus! Hear His words: "A new commandment I give to you, that you love one another, even as I have loved you, that you also love one another. By this all men will know that you are My disciples, if you have love for one another" (John 13:34–35; emphasis mine). This is my commandment, that you love one another, **just as I have loved you**" (John 15:12; emphasis mine).

Notice, however, that James equates the royal law with "loving your neighbor as you love yourself," not with "loving your neighbor as Jesus loves you." Actually, James is quoting from Leviticus 19, where God is giving Moses various laws for the congregation of the sons of Israel to follow in their relationships with one another. "You shall not take vengeance, nor bear any grudge against the sons of your people, but you shall love your neighbor as yourself; I am the Lord" (Leviticus 19:18). This gives *context and clarity* to this idea of loving our neighbors as we love ourselves.

How can loving others as we love ourselves be a good thing, especially in light of the fact that most (if not all) of us love ourselves so selfishly?

Taken out of context, the command to love your neighbor as you love yourself is more than frightening, especially in light of the way most of us so selfishly love ourselves. However, taken in context, the verse takes on a whole new meaning. Jesus said it like this: "Therefore, however you want people to treat you, so treat them, for this is the Law and the Prophets" (Matthew 7:12). As you can see, this attitude will eliminate partiality!

Notice, however, that Jesus raises the bar, per His usual modus operandi. He takes the law that God gave to Moses for the children of Israel, the law to which James refers—the royal law—and raises the standard far and above anything that any of us could ever reach, by simply replacing **as yourself** with **just as I have loved you.** "This is my commandment, that you love one another, just as I have loved you" (John 15:12; emphasis mine). As you can readily see, this drives us in hopeless desperation to Jesus because we simply cannot love another (even ourselves) the way He loves us.

To say, "You shall love your neighbor as yourself" is *not* the same as saying, "You shall love your neighbor as Jesus loves you." The standard of the latter is much higher than the standard of the former, so much higher that no one can reach it.

Even so, James tells us that we are doing well if we refrain from showing partiality by fulfilling the royal law, the law that tells us to love our neighbors as we love ourselves. The good news is this: we fulfill the royal law only when we have abandoned our efforts to meet either the Old Covenant standard (love your neighbor as yourself) or the New Covenant standard (love your neighbor as I love you) and are, thereby, driven to Jesus as our only hope.

How can we reconcile the fact that God has forgiven us for all of our sins and declared us to be as righteous as Jesus is righteous, with James's declaration that when we show partiality, the law convicts us as transgressors of the entire law?

The fact that the law convicts us as transgressors of the entire law is the very thing that gives meaning and significance to the grace and mercy that God has so freely bestowed upon us. Once again, this fact drives us to Jesus, who is our forgiveness and our righteousness.

In light of this, James encourages us to speak and to act as those who are to be judged by the law of liberty—the perfect law. "So speak and so act, as those who are to be judged by the law of liberty" (James 2:12). You see, the law of liberty is the perfect law, the law that sets us free from condemnation and judgment—the Law of the Spirit of Life in Christ Jesus. Obviously, the fact that the law convicts us as transgressors is precisely that which continually drives us to Jesus, who did for us what the law could never do, namely, fulfill the law's requirement in our behalf. "For what the Law could not do, weak as it was in the flesh, God did: sending His own Son in the likeness of sinful flesh and as an offering for sin, He condemned sin in the flesh, in order that the requirement of the Law might be fulfilled in us, who do not walk according to the flesh, but according to the Spirit" (Romans 8:3–4).

Notice this bit of really good news: just as we become guilty of the entire law as the result of our violating even one point of it, so has the requirement of the entire law been fulfilled in us as the result of Jesus's vicarious death and resurrection. "So then through one transgression there resulted condemnation to all men, even so through one act of righteousness there resulted justification of life to all men. For as through the one man's disobedience the many were made sinners, even so through the obedience of the One the many will be made righteous" (Romans 5:18–19).

Obviously, when we accept these tremendous truths, it follows that we should speak and act as those who will be judged by this law of liberty. In other words, we should treat others in the same way that God treats us—freely and lavishly bestowing mercy and grace. As you can see, the person who is fulfilling this "royal law" is, indeed, doing well, neither attempting to get revenge nor bearing grudges—treating others the way he would like to be treated.

Mercy does, indeed, triumph over judgment!

17
Faith and Works

"What use is it, my brethren, if a man says he has faith, but he has no works? Can that faith save him? If a brother or sister is without clothing and in need of daily food, and one of you says to them, 'Go in peace, be warmed and be filled,' and yet you do not give them what is necessary for their body, what use is that? Even so faith, if it has no works is dead, being by itself. But someone may well say, 'You have faith, and I have works; show me your faith without the works, and I will show you my faith by my works.' You believe that God is one. You do well; the demons also believe and shudder. But are you willing to recognize, you foolish fellow, that faith without works is useless? Was not Abraham our father justified by works, when he offered up Isaac his son on the altar? You see that faith was working with his works, and as a result of the works, faith was perfected; and the Scripture was fulfilled which says, 'And Abraham believed God, and it was reckoned to him as righteousness,' and he was called the friend of God. You see that a man is justified by works, and not by faith alone. And in the same way was not Rahab the harlot also justified by works, when she received the messengers and sent them out by another way? For just as the body without the spirit is dead, so also faith without works is dead" (James 2:14–26).

With all that can be said about grace, often at the expense of works, Paul does tell us that "we are God's workmanship, created in Christ Jesus for good works which God prepared beforehand, that we should walk in them" (Ephesians 2:10). To say that another way and to personalize it: God created me (a new creation) and placed me into Christ Jesus, in order that I might walk in the good works that He specifically prepared for me before the foundation of the world.

Furthermore, James tells us that faith without works is dead faith: "Even so, faith without works is dead, being by itself" (James 2:17). Interestingly, the examples he gives us are none other than Abraham and Rahab: "You see that faith was working with his works, and as a result of the works the faith was perfected" (James 2:22). "And in the same way was not Rahab the harlot also justified by works, when she received the messengers and sent them out by another way" (James 2:25).

James goes on to say this: "You see that man is justified by works and not by faith alone" (James 2:24). On the surface, this appears to contradict Paul when he said, "For by grace you have been saved through faith; and that not of yourselves, it is a gift of God; not as a result of works, that no one should boast" (Ephesians 2:8–9).

In my opinion, it is our strong performance mind-set regarding works that leads us to see these verses as contradictions, when in reality (as I hope to show), they fit together quite nicely.

In the first place, it is important to understand that there are two kinds of works: (1) "performance-based" works that are as a filthy garment to God (see Isaiah 64:6, Galatians 5:1–11, Hebrews 10:5–6), and (2) "grace-based" works that not only bring pleasure to God, but also demonstrate our faith in Him and our dependence upon Him (see Ephesians 2:10, Hebrews 9:13–14, and Colossians 1:9–10).

Abraham's obedience to God in sacrificing Isaac is a powerful demonstration of the aforementioned "grace-based" works. Obviously, his obedience not only brought great pleasure to God, but it also demonstrated his faith in God, as well as his utter dependence upon Him. He was undeniably walking in one of those works that God prepared beforehand (in advance) specifically for him. Because this entire episode was a shadow of Jesus and of His sacrificial death for mankind, we can safely assume that Abraham's obedience in walking through it not only brought much pleasure to God, but also demonstrated his ruthless trust (absolute dependence) in God as his provider and redeemer. Abraham knew (and he knew quite well) that God had to come through regarding His promise; otherwise, he was done—finished. "In hope against hope he believed, in order that he might become the father of many nations, according to that which had been spoken, 'So shall your descendents be.' And without becoming weak in faith, he contemplated his own body, now as good as dead since he was about a hundred years old, and the deadness of Sarah's womb; yet, with respect to the promise of God, he did not waver in unbelief, but grew strong in faith, giving glory to God, and being fully assured that what He has promised, He was able also to perform" (Romans 4:18–21).

Now, please notice that the scripture tells us that God reckoned Abraham righteous (justified him), not as the result of works but as the result of faith. If it had been otherwise, then Abraham would have had something about which he could boast, and that was not to be, unless he would boast in his self-righteousness. "For if Abraham was justified by works, he has something to boast about; but not before God. For what does the Scripture say? 'And Abraham believed God, and it was reckoned to him as righteousness'" (Romans 4:2–3). You see, Abraham was justified (made righteous) in order that he might walk in the grace-based works that God had previously prepared specifically for him. In other words, these works are the fruit of faith, not the other way around. Abraham would have never left Ur of the Chaldeans had God not first given him faith and had that faith not become trust—faith in action (obedience).

The point is this: faith precipitates trust (obedience)—i.e., it precipitates our walking in the specific grace-based works that God planned from the foundation of the world for each of us. Interestingly, these works are proof positive of not only our faith in Him but also our dependence upon Him for our own justification (righteousness).

Having established the above, I think we can now see more clearly just what James meant when he said that we are justified by works and not by faith alone. You see, these works are the fruit of faith in Jesus; consequently, we cannot have one without the other. On the other hand, faith without works is dead faith, and dead faith produces no good fruit—none whatsoever. To use the words of Martin Luther, "We are justified by faith alone but not by a faith that is alone." Living, abiding faith simply cannot exist apart from "grace-based" works—the works that God prepared beforehand for each of us.

As Paul said, we have been created in Christ Jesus for good works; however, until we cease striving and, thereby, end our efforts to do our own performance-based works, we will never walk in these good, grace-based works. Without the faith to trust our lives into His care, we will never walk in the works that He prepared beforehand; instead, our works will be limited to what we can accomplish in and through our own energies—performance-based works. In other words, we will never see the supernatural hand of God at work in our lives accomplishing His works and purposes. We will never see a "ram in a thicket."

Has His faith been perfected in your life? Can you honestly say that you are resting in His finished work and, consequently, not busying yourself with "performance-based" works? If your answers are in the affirmative, I can bet that you have already seen your "ram in the thicket," and I can also bet that you have found the peace that passes *all* understanding. There is nothing quite like watching His faith work itself out in your own life, and then seeing faith in action, as you trust Him to accomplish the works He prepared from the foundation of the world specifically for you.

18

A Perfect Conscience

> "Even so faith, if it has no works, is dead being by itself. But someone may well say, 'You have faith, and I have works; show me your faith without the works, and I will show you my faith by my works.' For just as the body without the spirit is dead, so also faith without works is dead" (James 2:17–18, 26).

If James is correct (and he is) and faith is dead unless it is accompanied by works, then, obviously, we should develop a clear and biblical understanding of "works." Interestingly, regardless of the types of works—dead works or living works, works of the flesh or works of the Spirit, works that offend God or works that please God, works that God prepared beforehand or works that we conjure as we journey—each of them can be placed in one of the following categories: performance-based works or grace-based works. Although it is obvious as to which of these categories of "works" is associated with dead faith, in my opinion the following text offers us a significant clue that facilitates our understanding of James's use of the word "works" in the aforementioned text. "Accordingly both gifts and sacrifices are offered which cannot make the worshipper perfect in conscience, since they relate only to food and drink and various washings, regulations for the body imposed until a time of reformation" (Hebrews 9:9–10).

In so many ways, the Day of Atonement (Yom Kippur) was an incredible day in the lives of the Jews; however, it was not without fault—serious fault. "But now He has obtained a more excellent ministry, by as much as He is also the mediator of a better covenant, which has been enacted on better promises. For if that first covenant had been faultless, there would have been no occasion sought for a second" (Hebrews 8:6–7).

For starters, the blood of bulls and goats *could not take sin away*, regardless of how perfect the animals might have been. "For it is impossible for the blood of bulls and goats to take away sins" (Hebrews 10:4).

In the second place, whatever level of efficacy the blood of these sacrificial animals might have had, it was at best only temporary and short-lived, as is evidenced by the Day of Atonement; once was definitely not enough. "For the Law, since it has only a shadow of the good things to come and not the very form of things, can never by the same sacrifices year by year, which they offer continually, make perfect those who draw near. Otherwise, would they not have ceased to be offered, because the worshipers, having once been cleansed, would no longer have had consciousness of sins?" (Hebrews 10:1).

In the third place, these sacrifices could *only* atone (cover) for sin; consequently, they could not deal with the root of sin—the Adamic man.

In the fourth place, these sacrifices could only atone (cover) sins already committed and, therefore, had no efficacy whatsoever for sins yet to be committed.

Finally and very significantly, the aforementioned limitations (faults) left the worshippers with a tremendous sense of guilt and condemnation—sin consciousness—and, therefore, having no clue as to a perfect conscience. As you might imagine, this guilt-ridden conscience produced legalism—striving to earn what Jesus died to give us—in its purest form, along with the accompanying dead works and, therefore, dead faith.

Interestingly, God built within the structure of the Day of Atonement (Yom Kippur) a method by which the Jews could, at least, temporarily deal with this resulting and dreaded sin consciousness—the scapegoat. After the high priest returned from the priestly service of sprinkling blood on the mercy seat, he would then (figuratively) place the sins of the people of Israel upon its head. At that point, someone who was standing in readiness would lead the scapegoat as far out into the wilderness as possible, in order to minimize the chances of the scapegoat's returning to the tabernacle with Israel's sins. When this was accomplished, the Israelites breathed a much-desired sigh of relief; albeit, a very temporary sigh, because the scapegoat was at best only a shadow of the substance that was to come.

Unfortunately, the fear that the scapegoat might return with Israel's sins, along with the fact that only "sins already committed" were involved in this atonement, left the worshippers in a constant state of sin consciousness. Consequently, they could never enjoy a perfect conscience. They lived in the fear that their sins would, indeed, find them out! "Then Aaron shall lay both of his hands on the head of the live goat, and confess over it all the iniquities of the sons of Israel, and all their transgressions in regard to all their sins; and he shall lay them on the head of the goat and send it away into the wilderness by the hand of a man who stands in readiness. And the goat shall bear on itself all their iniquities to a solitary land; and he shall release the goat in the wilderness" (Leviticus 16:21–22).

Surely our text makes *this* obvious: the gifts and sacrifices of the Old Covenant were never meant to remove sins because they related only to regulations concerning food and drink and various washings—regulations for the body that were in force *only* until a time of reformation, a time when things would be made correct (straight). The fact is the blood of bulls and goats cannot take sins away. "For it is impossible for the blood of bulls and goats to take away sins" (Hebrews 10:4).

Interestingly, the author is telling us what the gifts and sacrifices of the Old Covenant could *not* accomplish, in order to point us to the One who has accomplished those very things, one of the most significant of which is a perfect conscience. Contrary to popular opinion, there is no lasting victory for the Christian who lives with a consciousness of sin. In fact, he is no better off, regarding his being released from a guilty conscience, than were the Jews. In his mind, a perfect conscience is out of the question.

Having said that, what is meant by *a perfect conscience*? Verse 14 of this same chapter (10) opens the door for our answer: "How much more will the blood of Christ, who through the eternal Spirit offered Himself without blemish to God, cleanse your conscience from dead works to serve the living God?" (Hebrews 9:14; emphasis mine). Obviously, a perfect conscience is one that has been freed from guilt and condemnation, along with the debilitating, demoralizing stench of dead works. You see, a perfect conscience is free not only from dead works, but also from their influence! How? Through the blood of Christ!

In order to pursue our answer further, let us answer this question: What are *dead works*? Dead works are the works we do *not* to serve God but to serve ourselves—the works we attempt in order to earn His approval and acceptance, rather than trusting in His finished work. They are (without exception) acts of disobedience, and they can and often do include such "holy cows" as these (when they are done to serve the flesh, rather than to serve God): prayer, Bible study, fasting, attending church, memorizing scripture, feeding the poor, preaching, and even teaching Sunday school. These dead works are the works we do apart from faith (faith without works is dead faith) in the finished work that Jesus accomplished on the cross in our behalf.

Hebrews 10:2 makes the answer even more obvious: "Otherwise, would they not have ceased to be offered because the worshippers, having once been cleansed, would no longer have had consciousness of sins?" A perfect conscience is one that, as a result of the perfect efficacy of the sacrificial Lamb of God, the sacrifice that actually takes sin away, senses no need to return to the "altar of sacrifice" for more cleansings. Once is enough!

Surely, it is now obvious that the perfect conscience is the one that is no longer focused upon sin; instead, it is focused upon righteousness—the righteousness of God in Christ! What a difference this makes in the life of the believer, especially in his lasting victory over the guilt, power, and judgment of sin. This person no longer senses the need to perform for God in order to gain His acceptance, approval, and love—His conscience is perfect!

From a practical standpoint, what does this mean? How does this play itself out in the everyday life of the believer? In this way: the believer, who rests in the efficacy and finished (once-for-all-time) sacrifice of the Lamb of God, lives his life not in the *demoralizing* state of being conscious of sin, but in the *liberating* state of being conscious of righteousness (the righteousness of God in Christ), and He does so because:

1. He is convinced (by faith) that Jesus bore his sins in His body on the cross, eternally freeing him from guilt and condemnation.
2. He is convinced (by faith) that Jesus took his sins away, eternally removing them as far as the east is from the west.
3. He is convinced (by faith) that Jesus imputed His righteousness to him, leaving him without spot or blemish.

This man is free to walk in the specific and *good* works that God prepared beforehand, especially for him! "For we are His workmanship, created in Christ Jesus for good works, which God prepared beforehand, that we should walk in them" (Ephesians 2:10).

Now, back to James: "Even so faith, if it has no works, is dead being by itself" (James 2:17). Obviously, Martin Luther was correct: *We are justified by faith alone, but not by a faith that is alone.* Just as obviously, this justifying faith is always accompanied by grace-based works, the works that God graciously prepared and specifically tailored beforehand for each of us, the works that He exhibits only in the lives of those who experientially enjoy the perfect conscience that Jesus's vicarious sacrifice provides.

Without this perfect conscience, man will continue to live in fear of the wrath of God, always striving to come up with sacrifices sufficient to appease His anger, and producing in huge quantities the works of the flesh—dead works. "For if the blood of goats and bulls and the ashes of a heifer sprinkling those who have been defiled, sanctify for the cleansing of the flesh, **how much more** will the blood of Christ, who through the eternal Spirit offered himself without blemish to God, cleanse your conscience from dead works to serve the living God?" (Hebrews 9:13–14).

19

Let Not Many of You Become Teachers

> "Let not many of you become teachers, my brethren, knowing that as such we shall incur a stricter judgment" (James 3:1).

In my opinion, James had chapter 2, especially the last half of it, in mind when he penned our text. Actually, when I was preparing to present what James had to say about faith and works, I had this similar thought: what am I doing attempting to teach this? In the first place, the whole idea of faith and works is crucial to the truth of the gospel; both must be understood. In the second place, James makes it sound as if he is contradicting everything Paul had to say about the subject, and that muddiness must be clarified—made simple—which is not an easy task. In the third place, "faithfulness to correct doctrine" does not allow for compromise; consequently, justification by faith must be just that—justification by faith apart from works—regardless of the implications to the contrary that James made. Finally, because many perceive me as a God-called teacher of the gospel, I must be very careful to divide the entire Word of Truth correctly, not merely the piece that deals with faith and works; otherwise, I mislead my hearers/readers and, therefore, incur their strict judgment. To say the least, I understand why James warned that not many of us should become teachers.

Jesus, Himself, made this interesting statement concerning our being teachers in one of His confrontations with the scribes and Pharisees: "But do not be called Rabbi; for One is your Teacher, and you are all brothers" (Matthew 23:8). No, I do not believe that He was telling them (or us) that we should not teach; however, I do believe that He was making this point very clear: as a teacher, never set yourself above Him because He is *the* teacher. You might well say that you would never do that; however, when we take liberties with the scriptures, liberties, for example, that are designed to attract the masses, we are in fact placing ourselves above Him. The scribes and Pharisees did the same thing when they "taught as doctrines the precepts of men" (see Matthew 15:9b).

Paul does make it clear that teaching is a spiritual gift, a gift that the Holy Spirit uses; consequently, we do not want to allow James's caution to instill fear in us and, thereby, to prevent us from teaching. "And *God has appointed in the church*, first apostles, second prophets, third *teachers*, then miracles, then gifts of healings, helps, administrations, various kinds of tongues" (1 Corinthians 12:28; emphasis mine). To be sure, when God appoints someone in the church as a teacher, that appointment is serious business, but we must not allow its seriousness to cause us to run from it. For reasons beyond me, God has chosen to use some of us as teachers in His church and that is, indeed, a very high calling, a calling we should approach in reverence, but never in fear. You see, reverence approaches teaching from a God-centered perspective; whereas, fear approaches teaching from a self-centered perspective.

Although God has appointed teachers in the church, there are many who teach without such appointment. Sunday school is probably one of the most obvious examples. For as long as I can remember, Sunday school has been touted as one of the most important parts of church life, even an essential to spiritual health, but only God knows the extent of the spiritual abuse that has occurred as a result of erroneous teaching. This is not intended to imply that every Sunday school teacher is a heretic, because some are truly God-called and appointed; however, most merely adhere to a "quarterly" that is designed as propaganda for the particular denomination's growth. Furthermore, most of the teacher's preparation is done frantically on Saturday night in order to "get up a lesson" rather than out of desire to know and to impart truth.

To be sure, this is also true in pulpit preaching. I do not think it takes much insight to know that many, far too many, preachers are more interested in pleasing people than in teaching truth. The evidence is clear: all one has to do is to listen to the message being taught. Several years ago, I was involved in a theological conversation with a pastor concerning this very issue. I will never forget his comment: "I cannot teach what I really believe because I need this job."

As a result of this mentality, Jesus is seldom ever mentioned, and when He is, He is presented as someone far removed from who He really is. Furthermore, the gospel is so terribly distorted that Paul probably spends most of his heavenly days standing at the "pearly gate" entrance, shaking his fist in righteous indignation! As strange as it seems, especially in light of what I just said, Paul said this: "God was well-pleased through the foolishness of the message preached to save those who believe" (1 Corinthians 1:21b). Maybe there is hope, after all!

In view of James's caution, I do believe there are some truths regarding God-appointed teachers within the church that should be identified:

- Every believer is a God-appointed witness (see Acts 1:8), but not every believer is a God-appointed teacher. "All are not teachers, are they?" (1 Corinthians 12:29).

- Every God-appointed teacher is a serious student of God's Word, but not every serious student of God's Word is a God-appointed teacher, as some hold other appointments. "And God has appointed in the church, first apostles, second prophets, third teachers, then miracles, then gifts of healings, helps, administrations, various kinds of tongues" (1 Corinthians 12:28).

- Those who have not been so gifted and appointed by God should avoid placing themselves in the realm of the "few" to which James refers, especially in view of the stricter judgment.

- Every God-appointed teacher is well aware that *the* teacher is the Holy Spirit, that He is the revealer of truth. "But the Helper, the Holy Spirit, whom the Father will send in My name, He will teach you all things, and bring to your remembrance all that I said to you" (John 14:26).

- Every God-appointed teacher has the God-given desire to present Jesus as the centerpiece of his teaching. "In the beginning was the Word, and the Word was with God, and the Word was God. He was in the beginning with God. All things came into being by Him, and apart from Him nothing came into being that has come into being. In Him was life, and the life was the light of men" (John 1:1–4).

- Every God-appointed teacher is well aware that he has a teacher upon whom he is entirely dependent—Jesus.

- Every God-appointed teacher knows that the purpose of teaching is not to persuade others, but merely to present truth and allow the Holy Spirit to reveal it, according to His good pleasure.

- Every God-appointed teacher knows that truth is not a system of theology, or a mere dogma, but is a person— the person of Jesus.

There is another side of this proverbial coin called "teacher," and it is this: since James cautions that not many of us become teachers, it follows that each of us should be very careful as to whom we allow into our lives as teachers. From what I have been able to observe over the years, Christians, as a whole, are very reckless and careless when it comes to allowing spiritual teachers into their lives. For some reason, the charisma of the teacher seems to have more positive influence than does his ability and calling as a teacher.

It has amazed me for quite some time that so many sincere Christians not only spend hours listening to whomever the radio or television presents, but also accepting as truth everything that is said. There is no telling just how many times I have heard a believer say to me, "I really like him because he tells it like it is!" When I hear that, I always wonder if the "it" he is "telling like it is" is truth, and for good reason: if it is not truth, the person so intrigued is also so deceived!

It appears to me that every believer would have the gumption to check what is being taught against the truth of the scriptures and not, merely, to accept it at face value because it was taught by the Reverend Dr. Whing Ding Doozie. Unfortunately, far too many Christians are satisfied having someone spoon feed them what amounts to pious pablum, and that is tragic!

Let me encourage each of you to be as diligent in choosing your spiritual teachers as you are in choosing your physicians— even more so! I have never met anyone who would intentionally allow a "quack" physician to treat him or anyone he loved, for that matter, nor have I known many who would allow a legitimate physician to treat them without being certain that they are competent, skilled, and experienced—board certified, fellows, with much experience. Strangely, however, the very same folk often have no criteria regarding the teachers they allow to attend their spiritual health. The fact that they continue to live imprisoned lives, even though they have listened to hours of "truth" from their teacher(s), doesn't seem to awaken them at all.

To be sure, we must agree that James, in spite of Luther's accusation of it being a book of straw, is correct. Very few (only the God-appointed) should identify themselves as "teacher," and those who do should be careful to remember who *the* teacher really is—Jesus! However, those who wear the appointment and calling must be faithful to carry it out until the end—rightly dividing the Word of Truth—without regard to the mirrors of a thousand opinions. Furthermore, those being taught should take heed to James's caution as well, as there is much at stake— very much.

20

Stumbling

Interestingly, the scriptures make many metaphorical references (over one hundred) to "stumbling"; some having to do with mere stumbling, and some having to do with stumbling so as to fall, but all having to do with spiritual stumbling, as opposed to physical stumbling.

Before moving further into the text, it might serve us well to define what James means by "stumbling." For most of us, stumbling is primarily what we do when we are not paying attention to the path before us and trip over a rock, step in a hole, or get our foot caught in a vine. If we are fortunate, we manage somehow to catch ourselves and to remain erect; if not, we fall headlong onto whatever might be beneath us.

In the scriptures, however, stumbling is primarily what we do when truth offends us and we, therefore, reject it by refusing to submit to it. If we are fortunate, we manage somehow (the

Holy Spirit opens our eyes) to catch ourselves—recognize our error (confess), turn from it (repent), and embrace the truth (trust)—and to remain spiritually erect. If not, we fall, but never headlong. "The steps of a man are established by the Lord; and He delights in his way. When he falls, he shall not be hurled headlong; because the Lord is the One who holds his hand" (Psalm 37:23–24; emphasis mine). To be sure, we will stumble; however, we will never fall headlong and for this good reason: Jesus is holding our hands.

The best explicatory text I can think of is this: "The stone which the builders rejected, this became the very corner stone and a stone of stumbling and a rock of offense; for they stumble because they are disobedient to the word, and to this doom they were also appointed" (1 Peter 2:7b–8). Obviously, the people to whom Peter refers are those who were appointed to the doom of rejecting the Truth—Jesus—as opposed to a believer rejecting a portion of truth; consequently, those so appointed do fall headlong. Fortunately, however, believers are believers because God chose for us to accept and to embrace Jesus; consequently, we cannot fall headlong! He is holding our hands!

Interestingly, Jesus gave such significance to this idea of stumbling that He took the time to point out not only that our body members (hand, foot, and eye) play a major role in our propensity to stumbling, our failing to submit to truth, but also the seriousness of the consequences of our stumbling. "And if your hand causes you to stumble, cut it off; it is better for you to enter life crippled, than having your two hands, to go into hell into the unquenchable fire, where their worm does not die, and the fire is not quenched. And if your foot causes you to stumble, cut it off; it is better for you to enter life lame, than having your two feet, to be cast into hell, where their worm does not die, and the fire is not quenched. And if your eye causes you to stumble, cast it out; it is better for you to enter the kingdom of God with one eye, than having two eyes, to be cast into hell, where their worm does not die, and the fire is not quenched" (Mark 9:43–48; emphasis mine). Obviously, according to Jesus, it is better for us to lose our body members, any and all of them, than to continue stumbling, to continue refusing to submit to truth.

Please do not interpret this to mean that you would end up in hell (where the worm does not die, and the fire is not quenched), if you, as a believer, should stumble, even if you stumble many times per day! Jesus is not condemning stumbling believers to hell; much to the contrary, He is teaching that failing to submit to truth—stumbling—has dire consequences.

James indicates that we all stumble in many ways, which is, of course, true. The question, then, is this: in what ways do I stumble? In what ways am I refusing to submit to truth? Obviously, I cannot answer that for you; however, I can offer some of the truths of scripture, but keep in mind that you might stumble over them:

1. "Do not let kindness and truth leave you; bind them around your neck, write them on the tablet of your heart" (Proverbs 3:3). [Does this truth cause you to stumble, or are you submitting to it?]

2. "My son, do not reject the discipline of the Lord, or loathe His reproof, for whom the Lord loves he reproves, even as a father, the son in whom he delights" (Proverbs 3:11). [Does this truth cause you to stumble, or are you submitting to it?]

3. "The beginning of wisdom is: Acquire wisdom; and with all your acquiring, get understanding. Prize her, and she will exalt you; she will honor you if you embrace her. She will place on your head a garland of grace; she will present you with a crown of beauty" (Proverbs 4:7–9). [Does this truth cause you to stumble, or are you submitting to it?]

4. "Go to the ant, O sluggard, observe her ways and be wise" (Proverbs 6:6). [Does this truth cause you to stumble, or are you submitting to it?]

5. "Now therefore, my sons, listen to me, and pay attention to the words of my mouth. Do not let your heart turn aside to her ways, do not stray into her paths. For many are the victims she has cast down, and numerous are all her slain" (Proverbs 7:24–26). [Does this truth cause you to stumble, or are you submitting to it?]

6. "When pride comes, then comes dishonor, but with the humble is wisdom" (Proverbs 11:2). [Does this truth cause you to stumble, or are you submitting to it?]

7. "The way of a fool is right in his own eyes, but a wise man is he who listens to counsel" (Proverbs 12:15). [Does this truth cause you to stumble, or are you submitting to it?]

8. "Pride goes before destruction, and a haughty spirit before stumbling" (Proverbs 16:18). [Does this truth cause you to stumble, or are you submitting to it?]

9. "A good name is to be more desired than great riches, favor is better than silver and gold" (Proverbs 22:1). [Does this truth cause you to stumble, or are you submitting to it?]

10. "The rich rule over the poor and the borrower becomes the lender's slave" (Proverbs 22:7). [Does this truth cause you to stumble, or are you submitting to it?]

Obviously, this list could go on and on. However, may I simply suggest that you do your own inventory and make a list of the ways you are "stumbling," the ways you are refusing to submit to truth? It will be to your benefit, and that, I promise!

Now for the clincher! James makes this clear—very clear: of all the body members that might cause us to stumble, the tongue is the most difficult to bring into submission. In fact, not only does he tell us that no one can tame the tongue, he also tells us that it is full of deadly poison! "But no one can tame the tongue; it is a restless evil and full of deadly poison" (James 3:8). Obviously, since no one can tame it, and since it is full of deadly poison, it is, then, like a loaded and loose cannon in the hands of a fool, capable of doing much harm.

This is the point: Since no man can tame the tongue—bring it into submission to truth—it causes us (and others) much grief. Obviously, if the hand, foot, and eye cause us to stumble, the tongue does so even more because it makes evident that which fills the heart. "For the mouth speaks out of that which fills the heart" (Matthew 12:34). At the very least, this could make one a bit apprehensive not only about what comes out of his own mouth, but also about what comes out of the mouths of others—what he listens to. It makes one wonder if any of us ever speak truth—pure truth!

James reinforces this when he tells us that the man who does not stumble in what he says is a perfect man, able to bridle the whole body as well. To be sure, he closed the door on self-righteous perfection because no man is perfect in what he says—no man! Furthermore, he also makes it clear that no man can bridle his body—hand, foot, eye, or whatever. It simply will not happen because he cannot bring the tongue into submission to truth.

I find James's analogies intriguing:

1. He reminds us that although we can place a bit into a horse's mouth and, thereby, bridle (bring into submission) his whole body, there is no "bit" that effectively bridles the body of man.
2. He reminds us that, although huge ships are directed wherever the pilot might desire by small

rudders, even in strong winds, there is no "rudder" that effectively directs the course of man's life, even in times of calm.

3. He tells us that even though every species of beasts, birds, reptiles, and creatures of the sea is tamed by man, no man can tame the tongue. Sadly, we not only curse men with it, but also, with the very same tongue, we bless our Lord and Father. As James said, "These things ought not to be this way!" (James 3:10).

Like the small rudder that directs the huge ship, so also is the tongue a small part of the body; yet, it is set among our members as that which defiles the entire body, and sets on fire the course of our lives, and is set on fire by hell. "So also the tongue is a small part of the body, and yet it boasts of great things. Behold, how great a forest is set aflame by such a small fire!" (James 3:5b).

Once again, James is correct! "If anyone does not stumble in what he says, he is a perfect man, able to bridle the whole body as well" (James 3:2). Interestingly, however, and in light of all the negative things that James says about the tongue, in spite of the sense of hopelessness that his message brings, he does bring into his message this ray of hope: "My brethren, these things ought not to be this way" (James 3:10b). In other words, there is a way out, there is another option, there is a road to victory, and there is a way to overcome! What, pray tell is it?

As I said in my commentary of chapter 1, James knew a secret that few people of the religious world will never know because they are too self-centered, and this is it: *when relationship with the Father, Son, and Holy Spirit (the vertical) and relationship with others within the Body of Christ (the horizontal) become paramount in our hearts, something happens to our tongues.* Remember this: "For the mouth speaks out of that which fills the heart" (Matthew 12:34). To be sure, the mouth does speak out of the abundance of the heart! In other words, our only hope is for the transforming work of the Holy Spirit to be accomplished in our lives, the work that causes us to submit to truth, however painful and distasteful it might be, and, thereby, to prevent our stumbling, our being offended by the very truth that not only sheds light onto our pathways but also sets us free to trust Him, even in the dark.

21
The Fires of the Tongue

"So also the tongue is a small part of the body, and yet it boasts of great things. Behold, how great a forest is set aflame by such a small fire! And the tongue is a fire, the very world of iniquity; the tongue is set among our members as that which defiles the entire body, and sets on fire the course of our life, and is set on fire by hell" (James 3:5–6).

Having seen pictures of the blazing, roaring forest fires that have occurred at various locations around our nation, we are all aware of their devastation. Without exception, these terribly destructive fires are started by relatively small flames—a camper's match, an arsonist's torch, a smoker's cigarette butt, or a thunderstorm's lightning bolt. Once started, however, their destruction is widespread and merciless, their course is relentlessly pursued, and nothing is spared their fierce rage. The devastation that is left behind is incomprehensible—acres and acres of blackened earth, the cremated remains of innocent people and animals, the smoke-stained rubble of once-beautiful houses, and the charred stubble of once-beautiful, pristine forests.

Interestingly, James compares the tongue with one of these small, devastating flames. "Behold, how great a forest is set aflame by such a small fire" (verse 5b). Although I think most of us have a very clear picture of the terrible devastation a small blaze can bring, I do not believe we have as clear a picture of the magnitude of the devastation the tongue can bring, as is evidenced by the fact that most of us are much more careful and prophylactic in the way we handle fire, even a small flame, than we are in the way we handle our words—what we say. For example, on the one hand, none of us would think of abandoning a burning campfire or throwing a lighted cigarette onto the dry roadside grass. On the other hand, however, most of us think nothing about abandoning all reason and speaking a "burning" word about another or judging another guilty and condemned, oftentimes without so much as a shred of evidence.

The fact is, if we really believe that the tongue is a fire, a fire that is set on fire by hell, a fire that defiles the entire body, a fire that sets on fire the course of our lives, a fire that leaves much more devastation than any forest fire could ever leave, then, surely, we would at the very least be as careful with our words as we are with fire. I am fully convinced of this: if any one of us were given the opportunity to see the devastation the fires of our own tongues have left in their path, we would be astonished and horrified, even more than we would be at seeing the devastation of all the forest fires that have ever burned.

The Fire of Heresy

It is for this good reason that the fire of heresy is first on my list of the fires of the tongue: without question, it leaves the most destructive devastation of all the fires set on fire by hell! I truly wish I had kept a record of the number of times I have counseled someone who was the victim of heretical teaching. I well remember the women who came to me because of the burden they were carrying as the result of (1) having been taught that pleasing God required that their "quivers" be filled with children, and (2) having been taught that Christian couples must not use any birth control, other than the "birth control" taught by the Old Testament, which left sex *only* for the times when the woman was most fertile.

I also remember the weary and devastated wives who came to me as the result of having been taught that they were to live in submission to their abusive husbands. I could never forget the shamed adulterers who came to me as the result of having been taught that there is no forgiveness for this sin, and the angry divorced people who came to me as the result of having been taught that God hates divorced people. To be sure, I cannot omit the men and women involved in affairs, who came to me as the result of having been taught that Christians cannot have affairs.

As you might imagine, this list goes on and on; however, let me simply say this: there is no devastation like the devastation the fire of heresy leaves in its path—the charred remains of the very people for whom Jesus died. I am so glad that I know that He makes "dry bones" live again, that His finished work will always prevail, even in the face of heresy!

The Fire of Gossip

In all probability, my role as a pastor has exacerbated my awareness of the rampant virus of gossip that exists within the Body of Christ. Gossip has one goal and only one goal—to exalt the gossiper at the expense of the victim. One of its favorite breeding places is the small group prayer meeting, where confidential things are shared, as matters of prayer. Of course, it also has other favorite breeding grounds—too many to mention. Admittedly, there is sometimes a fine line that one must respect; however, anytime I tell someone something about another that exalts me at their expense, I am gossiping—tale bearing!

Interestingly, gossip is almost always distorted truth. For example, someone tells you that James and his wife had a fuss the other night; however, by the time you get around to telling someone else (usually sooner rather than later), James is abusing his wife. As another example, someone tells you that Sally's son, Alfred, is getting married to a young woman of ill-repute; however, by the time you get around to telling someone else (usually sooner rather than later), Alfred's fiancé is pregnant, and they are "having to get married." One final example, someone tells you that Jane is having an affair with a married man; however, by the time you get around to telling someone else (usually sooner rather than later), Jane has been reduced to a whore, who deserves to be stoned to death. To be sure, distorted truth is no truth at all; however, it is a useful tool for the gossiper, who by the way has no respect at all for truth! The devastation *The Fire of Gossip* leaves in its path—the charred debris of ruined, bankrupt lives—is a sight no one should ever have to witness.

The Fire of Judgment

If Jesus ever made anything crystal clear it is this: we are not to judge one another; however, we seem to have a difficult time practicing His directive. "Do not judge lest you be judged. For in the way you judge, you will be judged; and by your standard of measure, it will be measured to you. And why do you look at the speck that is in your brother's eye, but do not notice the log that is in your own eye?" (Matthew 7:1–3).

In our self-centered state of mind, it is very difficult even to imagine that we could possibly be guilty of the very same things for which we judge another. For whatever it might be worth, this is what Paul had to say: "Therefore you are without excuse, every man of you who passes judgment, for in that you judge another, you condemn yourself; for you who judge practice the same things" (Romans 2:1).

The fire of judgment burns with almost the same intensity as the fire of heresy, as is evidenced by the devastation it brings, not so much to those who are judged, but to the one who judges. I might add that we all judge with unrighteous judgment. This is the fact of the matter: there is but one righteous judge, and He is God. "And the Heavens declare His righteousness, for God Himself is judge" (Psalm 50:6). In His incredible wisdom, God did not see fit to design His children to be judges; instead, He chose to reserve that for Himself. In case you have not noticed, Jesus even distanced Himself for judging. Notice what He said: "For God did not send the Son into the world to judge the world, but that the world should be saved through Him" (John 3:17).

I have often wondered just how many of God's elect the people of the church have judged unfit and, therefore, condemned them to death. I wonder even more when these self-appointed judges will realize that they are the guilty, that they are the ones with the flame that is set on fire by hell, the flame that defiles the entire body. The devastation left in their path is, indeed, beyond belief because its victims are not the ones they judged "unfit" but themselves. To be sure, they will see the massacre—bloodshed, slaughter, butchery—but all too late. These profane, self-centered, self-appointed judges will have been judged—righteously!

The Fire of Truth Spoken without Love

There is nothing quite like the discovery of truth, especially to the one who is seeking hard after it, be it medical truth, historical truth, forensic truth, theological truth, or any other kind of truth. Oftentimes, however, when truth is discovered, it is not at all what we wanted to find. For example, one's physical person is sick but the reason eludes everyone, and the person's situation worsens. Finally, the right tests are done, and the truth is made evident—terminal cancer. Obviously, this was not the truth the person wanted to hear, regardless of how sensitively it might have been spoken to him. Irrespective of the love that might have been conveyed in telling this person this truth, his immediate reaction is one of denial, then anger, then tears, then, hopefully, resolution.

All too often, what follows is something like this: "I told you over and over that those cigarettes would kill you but you would not quit. Now look at what you have done! You are going to die and leave me to deal with everything." To be sure, what is being said is truth, real truth; however, it is spoken not in love but in anger.

Admittedly, this might be an extreme example, but most of us are very familiar with many not-so-extreme examples: the way we speak truth to our spouses, to our children, to those who offend us, and to those who threaten us, to mention a few.

Again, the path of destruction is wide and devastating, filled with the charred remains of rejected children, lonely wives, hurting husbands, and who knows who else. Truth is incredibly good and freeing—liberating; yet, when it is spoken without love, it can and often does bring death. The very truth that was designed to set us free, when spoken without love, imprisons and destroys. For example, the truth that God hates divorce, when spoken without love, comes across as God hates those who divorce and that imprisons and destroys—always!!

In conclusion, listen to these remarkable and encouraging words of Jesus: "And these signs will accompany those who have believed: in My name they will cast out demons, they will speak with new tongues" (Mark 16:17).

22

The Wisdom that Comes from Above

"Who among you is wise and understanding? Let him show by his good behavior his deeds in the gentleness of wisdom. But if you have bitter jealousy and selfish ambition in your heart, do not be arrogant and so lie against the truth. This wisdom is not that which comes down from above, but is earthly, natural, demonic. For where jealousy and selfish ambition exist, there is disorder and every evil thing. But the wisdom from above is first pure, then peaceable, gentle, reasonable, full of mercy and good fruits, unwavering, without hypocrisy. And the seed whose fruit is righteousness is sown in peace by those who make peace" (James 3:13–18).

Obviously, it does not require a PhD to know that there are two very distinct kinds of wisdom—the wisdom of the world and the wisdom of God. Strangely, however, most people see the wisdom of God as foolishness and the wisdom of the world as true wisdom. This is certainly evidenced by the sheer numbers of decisions and choices we make as we journey through this life, decisions that are in diametric opposition to the dictates of the wisdom of God. For example, the wisdom of God says this: "Actually, then, it is already a defeat for you, that you have lawsuits with one another. Why not rather be wronged? Why not rather be defrauded? On the contrary, you yourselves wrong and defraud, and that your brethren" (1 Corinthians 6:7–8). Just how many Christians follow this wisdom? Obviously, very few and the reason is simple: the wisdom of the world sounds much more practical and logical; in fact, to the person who is unable to see, this wisdom sounds nonsensical!

Having said that, what, exactly, is wisdom? To what is James referring by his reference to wisdom? In the New Testament, two words translate as wisdom—σοφια and φρονησισ. The former (the one used in our text) being insight into the true nature of things; whereas, the latter being the ability to discern modes of action—the practical application of the former. As we examine some of the various texts in which σοφια is used (Matthew 13:54; Mark 6:2: Luke 2:40, 52; Romans 11:33; 1 Corinthians 1:21, 24, 30; 2:7; 12:8; Ephesians 3:10; Colossians 2:3; Revelation 7:12) it becomes obvious that both are necessary and essential, one seldom being seen without the other.

Interestingly, in our text σοφια is used to translate both the wisdom that is from above—the wisdom of God—and the wisdom that is earthly, natural, and demonic. Notice how James differentiates them: "This wisdom (the wisdom that is centered in selfish ambition) is not that which comes down from above, but is earthly, natural, demonic" (verse 15; parenthesis mine). In other words, this wisdom, this self-centered insight into the true nature of things, results in modes of action—practical applications—that are purely selfish and, therefore, ungodly and foolish. Take another look at our previous example: this wisdom—the wisdom of the world—looks at this and says, "Because of the nature of this offense, you are justified in taking your brother to court!" It might seem "right" and it might feel "right," but in the end, it is the wisdom of the world—earthly, natural, and demonic!

Notice how James opens this section of chapter three: "Who among you is wise and understanding?" (James 3:13a). In other words, who among you has not only the ability to see into the true nature of things, but also the ability to discern modes of action that are coincident with godliness? This, he says, is how you can recognize the wise and understanding: "Let him show by his good behavior his deeds in the gentleness of wisdom" (verse 13b). In other words, the man with wisdom *and* understanding can be easily identified; what he does and the way he does it make him obvious.

You see, there are many people who have wisdom; however, they have no clue as to how to apply it in everyday living. It is my guess that every Christian has enough of God's wisdom to know that idol worship is utterly foolishness and equally sinful; however, few have any clue as to the practical application of this wisdom. As a result, many Christians are idolaters—self-worshipers rather than worshipers of the One True God.

Furthermore, I would like to believe that most Christians have enough of God's wisdom to know that Jesus perfectly and permanently dealt with our sin problem through His vicarious death on the cross; however, few have any clue as to the practical application of this wisdom. The epidemic of judging and condemning that is rampant within the church today evidences this.

Thankfully, if you look closely enough, you will discover that God has very carefully placed those with wisdom and understanding along the path of life, those who not only are able to see into the real nature of things but also are able to discern proper modes of action. When you are privileged to meet one of these wise men, take the time to look at what he is doing, examine how he is doing it, and listen, carefully, to what he is saying. In all probability, he is a messenger of God to you at precisely the correct time.

Obviously, this is noteworthy: "The wisdom from above is first pure, then peaceable, gentle, reasonable, full of mercy and good fruits, unwavering, without hypocrisy" (verse 17). I find it interesting that oftentimes the wisdom of the world appears to be much purer, gentler, more peaceable, and, certainly, more reasonable than the wisdom of God. Furthermore, the wisdom of the world oftentimes appears to be much more merciful than the wisdom of God, to bear much better fruit than the wisdom of God, to be much less wavering than the wisdom of God, and, certainly, to be without hypocrisy. If this were not true, we would be much more prone to follow the wisdom of God than we are to follow the wisdom of the world! How easily are we deceived!

Regardless of appearances, the wisdom of the world is foolishness, make no mistake! Listen to these words of Paul: "Who is the wise man? Where is the scribe? Where is the debater of this age? Has not God made foolish the wisdom of the world? For since in the wisdom of God the world through its wisdom did not come to know God, God was well pleased through the foolishness of the message preached to save those who believe. For indeed Jews ask for signs, and Greeks search for wisdom; but we preach Christ crucified, to Jews a stumbling block, and to Gentiles foolishness, but to those who are the called, both Jews and Greeks, Christ the power of God and the wisdom of God. Because the foolishness of God is wiser than men, and the weakness of God is stronger than men. For consider your calling, brethren, that there were not many wise according to the flesh, not many mighty, not many noble; but god has chosen the foolish things of the world to shame the wise, and God has chosen the weak things of the world to shame the things that are not, that He might nullify the things that are, that no man should boast before God" (1 Corinthians 1:20–30).

23

The Source of Quarrels and Conflicts

"What is the source of quarrels and conflicts among you? Is not the source your pleasures that wage war in your members?" (James 4:1).

Sadly, the church, much more so than the world, has always been a fertile breeding ground for quarrels and conflicts. From all I have been able to see (up close and personal), the people of the world get along with each other much better than the people of the church. Surely, we all must wonder how those of us who have been blessed with so much love, forgiveness, mercy, and grace have such a difficult time giving the same to others. Of all the people on earth, we should be the ones who live in harmony and love; however, that is not the picture others see when they look at our lives. This is probably the main reason most evangelism is merely Christians moving from one church to another, rather than lost people coming into the church. To be honest, I cannot blame them for their reluctance to join us; after all, why would anyone want to leave the relative peace and harmony of the world to become involved with the most difficult people on the planet?

Although I have seen local churches experience conflict-free, quarrel-free periods, most of them have been short-loved—very short-lived! Unfortunately, when conflicts and quarrels surface, they extract a terrible toll from those involved—a root of bitterness springs up, and many are defiled. Only Heaven knows how many of God's people have been wounded and left to die as the direct result of quarrels and conflicts within the Body of Christ. Sadly, most of them are committed never to return to church. Fortunately (and I am very glad I know this), God causes all things to work together for good to those who love Him, to those who are called according to His purpose! Somehow, even in the quarrels and conflicts, God is doing a good thing, a very good thing. Let us pray that we have eyes that see and ears that hear!

This is James's question: "What is the *source* of quarrels and conflicts among you?" (James 4:1a).

This is James's answer: "Is not the source your pleasures that wage war in your members?" (James 4b).

Note the Amplified Bible's translation of this question and answer: "What leads to strife (discord and feuds) and how do conflicts (quarrels and fightings) originate among you? Do they not arise from your sensual desires that are ever warring in your bodily members?" (James 4:1b).

Interestingly, in the previous chapter (3:14–16) James talks about "bitter jealousy" and "selfish ambition," and he tells us that where these exist there is disorder and every evil thing! Obviously, these two passages are linked, and for good reason: "bitter jealousy" and "selfish ambition" are the two sensual desires from which every conflict and every quarrel is derived. Note, too, that the Amplified Bible indicates our sensual desires are ever warring in our bodily members. Ironically, it is, therefore, safe to assume that there is a never-ending struggle/conflict within our own bodily members, a struggle between the flesh and the Spirit, a struggle that will remain with us until we get Home. Our sensual desires will always be in conflict with the desires of the Spirit, and that we cannot change; however, struggle and conflict do not necessarily mean defeat. Surely, it is possible for the Spirit to win, and to do so, even on a consistent basis! Actually, He has already won, but we have a difficult time appropriating the fact that He has. Instead, we choose to allow bitter jealousy and selfish ambition to rule, and when we do, the inner-struggle/conflict that we are experiencing begins to spew onto other members of the Body of Christ, and oftentimes the aforementioned root of bitterness springs up, and by it many are defiled.

What is really going on when we choose to allow our sensual desires (bitter jealousy and selfish ambition) to rule? Without exception, rather than trusting His provision, we are attempting to satisfy our God-given hunger and thirst for righteousness with something that will never satisfy.

Let us look at two examples:

When Christians Are Unfaithful

Frank and Jane, a Christian couple, have been married for twenty-five years, when Sally, who is also a Christian, comes to work in Frank's office. She unknowingly and unwittingly begins to meet the needs Frank has longed for Jane to meet most of their married life. As Frank warmly responds to Sally, she is drawn to him, perceiving that he is meeting the needs she has longed for her husband to meet; thus is the beginning of an emotional affair that, soon thereafter, becomes a full-blown sexual affair.

Obviously, both Frank and Sally are allowing their sensual desires to rule; albeit, the Spirit is very much alive, actively purposing to convince them of their righteousness—the ever-raging war between the flesh and the Spirit. Unfortunately, they perceive the Spirit's response to be convicting, condemning, and judging. Consequently, rather than running to the Holy Spirit with their sin, they choose to justify it by convincing themselves not only that their mates have deprived them of the things that are really needful in life, but also that this new relationship will fill all of their emptiness. This gives birth to a life of fantasy—believing that my way is better than God's way—by which they are convinced that they would be much happier if they divorced their mates and married each other. Obviously, it never dawns on them that God has a higher purpose for their lives than mere happiness, and that purpose is for them to find ultimate fulfillment in Jesus.

As you might expect, one of Jane's friends, who also works at Frank's office, picks up on their relationship and calls Jane to inform her of what is happening between Frank and Sally. Surely, it is obvious that the vomitus that is about to spew over other members of the Body of Christ, by way of the ensuing quarrels and conflicts, is quite viral, and devastatingly so.

At this point, I do not think it takes a rocket scientist to realize that James is right on target when he answers his own question: "Is not the source of the quarrels and conflicts among you your pleasures that wage war in your members? Do they not arise from your sensual desires that are ever warring in your bodily members?" (James 4:1).

An Unhappy Sunday School Teacher

Martha had been the youth teacher in a local church for many, many years, and as is sometimes the case, this teaching position was feeding her need to be loved and accepted, as well as giving her a sense of value and belonging. As you might imagine, this position was very valuable to her, and she had no intentions of allowing anyone to take it away! Unknowingly and unwittingly, when the Nominating Committee met, the new pastor made several recommendations concerning church leadership, not the least of which was that another person be given the opportunity to teach the youth. To be sure, this precipitated significant quarreling and conflict within that part of the Body of Christ. To say that "bitter jealousy" and "selfish ambition" ensued would be putting it mildly!

In a very short time, Martha had made her case with several of her close friends and set out on a mission to destroy anyone and everyone who disagreed with her—especially this new pastor. Of course, the new pastor began fervently to pray this very specific prayer: *Lord, please remove this Jezebel from our midst before she destroys this part of the Body of Your Son!* (Actually, his fervency was short-lived because he soon heard another pastor say this: *If you have someone in your church, who is determined to destroy it, do not pray for God to remove him/her because He will, and He will send someone worse!* Thus, *that* prayer quickly ended!)

Anyway, it does not take too many "smarts" to realize that the source of these quarrels and conflicts was, indeed, this woman's sensual desires, desires that were ever warring with the Spirit. I am convinced that in the beginning she believed she was doing the "right" thing. I am also convinced that when it became obvious to everyone that she was not doing the "right" thing, she continued to believe that she was and, therefore, continued the struggle until she finally left the church.

The division and death that these quarrels and conflicts wrought were devastating to many of God's people; however, it soon became obvious that God really does cause all things to work together for good to those who love Him and are the called according to His purpose, as that part of the Body of Christ began to flourish and grow, bearing lasting fruit.

Surely, each of us is asking this question: What does it take to get us to the place where we allow the Holy Spirit to win over the desires of the flesh? I think the Amplified Bible answers this question as well as it can be answered, and I might point out that it has much more to do with what He does than it has to do with what we do: "But He gives us more and more grace [power of the Holy Spirit, to meet this evil tendency and all others fully]. That is why He says, God sets Himself against the proud and haughty, but gives grace [continually] to the lowly—those who are humble-minded [enough to receive it]. So be subject to God. Stand firm against the devil; resist him and he will flee from you" (James 4:6–7, Amplified Bible).

How does this work itself out in our lives? To those who recognize their utter helplessness to conquer their sensual desires on their own—i.e., those who are humble enough to receive—He gives (releases) more and more grace, especially the grace to allow the power of the Holy Spirit to do what only He can do—make us more than conquerors. When He brings us to this place (which is the only way we can get there), and we humbly receive this grace, it is then and only then that we will resist the devil and submit to God. You see, He brings us to that place of humility, that place where we are willing to receive whatever it takes, and when He does, He gives us more and more grace, specifically the grace to resist the devil and to stand firm in submission to Him. All His doing, not ours!

24

When We Get What We Desire

"You are jealous and covet [what others have] and your desires go unfulfilled; [so] you become murderers. [To hate is to murder as far as your hearts are concerned.] You burn with envy and anger and are not able to obtain [the gratification, the contentment, and the happiness that you seek], so you fight and war. You do not have because you do not ask. [Or] you do ask [God for them] and yet fail to receive, because you ask with wrong purpose and evil, selfish motives. Your intention is, [when you get what you desire] to spend it in sensual pleasures. You [are like] unfaithful wives [having illicit love affairs with the world] and breaking your marriage vow to God! Do you not know that being the world's friend is being God's enemy? So whoever chooses to be a friend of the world takes his stand as an enemy of God. Or do you suppose that the Scripture is speaking to no purpose that says, The Spirit Whom He has caused to dwell in us yearns over us—and he yearns for the Spirit [to be welcome]—with a jealous love? But He gives us more and more grace [power of the Holy Spirit, to meet this evil tendency and all others fully]. This is why He says, God sets Himself against the proud and haughty, but gives grace [continually] to the lowly—those who are humble [enough to receive it]" (James 4:2–6, Amplified Bible).

One of the most encouraging passages in all of scripture is the one that tells us of Jesus's experience in the Garden of Gethsemane. As you remember, what He desired for Himself was at odds with what God desired for Him. "And He went a little beyond them, and fell on His face and prayed, saying, 'My Father, if it is possible, let this cup pass from Me; **yet not as I will, but as Thou wilt**'" (Matthew 26:39; emphasis mine); "Abba! Father! All things are possible for Thee; remove this cup from Me; yet not what I will, but what Thou wilt" (Mark 14:36; emphasis mine); "And being in agony he was praying fervently; and his sweat became like drops of blood, falling down upon the ground" (Luke 22:44; emphasis mine).

I used the word "encouraging" because Jesus's own struggle with God's will for Him lets me know that my struggles with His will for me do not render me faithless and worthless. Like Jesus, in the end, I know that God's will is always the best for me and for everyone involved; however, getting to that place of "yet not as I will but as Thou wilt" is never easy. To be honest, at times it seems impossible for me; however, I must quickly point out that it is this very struggle—the struggle to trust God when what I desire for myself is at odds with what He desires for me—that verifies and confirms my faith!

Jesus's experience in Gethsemane illustrates this. He was experiencing what was probably the most difficult time of His life, even sweating drops of blood. However, He was doing so not because He was faithless, but because He was filled with faith, absolutely convinced not only of His Father's righteousness, but also of His faithfulness. He knew beyond any shadow of doubt that His Father was doing a good thing, painful, but good, nevertheless. He also knew, just as surely, that His Father would see Him through, even to the resurrection! Even so, He struggled—really struggled—to submit to His Father's will, and in doing so, He evidenced His faith.

All of that to say this: we jealously covet what others have, but our desires go unfulfilled; we burn with envy and anger, but we are unable to obtain the gratification, contentment, and happiness we seek. In the end, we find ourselves murdering (hating is murder), fighting, and warring against the very members of Christ's Body. Tragically, when we finally get what we want, we spend it (not necessarily money) on sensual pleasures! What is wrong with us? Why is it so difficult for us to learn from our mistakes? Why do we insist on having our own way, rather than submitting to God's way? Why is it so difficult for us to pray, "Not my will but Thine be done?" Why does God refuse to give to us what we so desperately desire?

First, according to James, we do not have because we do not ask; however, more frequently, we do not have because we ask with wrong motives—the satisfying of our own sensual desires. As you remember, Israel grew tired of God's provision and began to complain to Moses, expressing not only their weariness with manna, but also their desire for meat. To make a long story short, God granted them what they desired (or what they thought they desired), and, well, you know the rest of the story. I am really thankful that God does not grant us everything we think we want. The stench of rotting quail would probably be a welcomed aroma, should He choose to do so!

Second, our being so friendly with the world makes us like adulteresses. We are like unfaithful wives having illicit love affairs with the world, breaking our marriage vow to God, which by the way, makes me very thankful that the success of the New Covenant is dependent upon His faithfulness, not mine! Fortunately, the New Covenant is a covenant between God and Jesus; consequently, I cannot break it, even though it sometimes appears that I have! Even when I do the very thing that would normally be considered a breach of the covenant, I have an advocate with the Father—Jesus Christ, the Righteous One, who always intercedes for me. "My little children, I am writing these things to you that you may not sin. And if anyone sins, we have an Advocate with the Father, Jesus Christ the righteous" (1 John 2:1). "And in the same way the Spirit also helps our weakness; for we do not know how to pray as we should, but the Spirit Himself intercedes for us with groaning too deep for words" (Romans 8:26).

Third, we are not convinced that the scriptures are absolute truth, nor are we convinced of their authority over our lives. Consequently, we often deceive ourselves into believing that we have a better way than God's way.

Admittedly, there are some questions for which the scriptures give us no answers. For example, the scriptures do not give you the best route to travel from Macon to Atlanta; you will need to check with AAA to get that answer. However, God has used the scriptures to make some things very clear—unmistakably clear—and we would profit not only from knowing what they are—absolute truth—but also by living in obedience to them—giving them authority over our lives.

For example, God has made it clear—unmistakably clear—that we are to walk in relationships of integrity. "A new commandment I give to you, that you love one another, even as I have loved you, that you also love one another" (John 13:34). Consequently, when we find ourselves compromising our integrity in order to get what we want, in order to satisfy one of our sensual desires, we can rest assured that we are struggling not only with the absolute truth of the scriptures, but also with its authority over our lives.

Finally, we have very little idea of just how jealously the Spirit, whom He made to dwell in us, desires us, even yearns for us! His desire for us was one of the three things that motivated Jesus to pray the "not My will but Thy will" prayer! The other two, of course, being (1) His love for His Father, and (2) His desire to please Him—in everything!

Of this I am convinced: the Holy Spirit uses the experiences of life to bring us to our own places of crushing, our own Gethsemane experiences. He very carefully leads us through various experiences of His own design, experiences that ultimate bring us to that place where we, too, must choose not only to release our own sensual desires, but also to submit to His sovereign plan for our lives.

How thankful I am that He does, indeed, give more and more grace (the Holy Spirit's power that enables us to release and to submit) to those who are humble enough to receive it. I might add this: those who are humble enough to receive it are those who have found themselves "sweating drops of blood" in their own places of crushing, their own Gethsemane.

By the way, contrary to what we might think and feel, God is always giving us that which we so passionately and desperately desire—intimacy with Jesus. Unfortunately, however, the journey to and through Gethsemane takes a while, and in the journey, our true desires often become clouded, even as Jesus's desires became clouded, and what we think we desire is not really what we desire.

25

Humility: How I Achieved It

"Humble yourselves in the presence of the Lord, and He will exalt you" (James 4:10).

Somewhere along the way, each of us has heard mention of the well-known book *Humility and How I Achieved It*. The author (for obvious reasons) seems to prefer stealth and, consequently, never reveals himself. However, I am going to "let the cat out of the bag" and reveal his identity—any Pelagian[4] or semi-Pelagian Protestant, most of whom you will recognize as run-of-the-mill Baptists, Methodists, Presbyterians, Lutherans, Episcopalians, Evangelicals, and Independents. And let us not

---

4 Although a priest, Pelagius (354–418) was a Celtic monk and a highly respected spiritual leader for both laymen and clergy. He firmly believed in the individual and in his ability to better himself as a spiritual being. The view of Pelagius and his followers firmly held to the doctrine of the free will of man and the innate goodness of nature, which, they claimed, was not corrupted but only modified by sin. Such a stand put them in direct opposition to their great antagonist, Augustine.

forget the Roman Catholics and Jews. This is evidenced by their insistence on adulterating the gospel with works, thereby exalting themselves. To say that another way, it is evidenced by their resistance to being humbled by another, especially by God.

Ironically, when we see true humility exhibited *in another person* (Jesus, for example), we are drawn to him, as a thirsty person is drawn to water. However, we typically view *our demonstrating humility* as a flaw that exposes our weaknesses and causes others to reject us. In order to cope with this perceived rejection, we clothe our pride in the self-made garments of humility that the followers of Pelagius sell—free will, morality, obedience, faithfulness, righteousness, and temperance, to name a few. With these "weapons of warfare" in hand, we set out as "soldiers of the cross" to "win the world for Jesus" and, thereby, to demonstrate our humility, as we "sacrifice everything" for Him and for His cause. Obviously, this proves to be self-righteousness—man exalting himself above God (pride in its purest form)—and, consequently, sets the stage for the ensuing humility that God accomplishes in the lives of those who exalt themselves. "And whoever exalts himself shall be humbled; and whoever humbles himself shall be exalted" (Matthew 23:12).

Interestingly, James anticipated our false humility, which is nothing less than pride in its purest form, and encouraged us to humble ourselves in the presence of the Lord. It is one thing for us to willingly humble ourselves before Almighty God, but it is quite another when Almighty God chooses to humble us. When we humble ourselves, He exalts us; however, when we refuse to humble ourselves, well, you know the rest!

Having said all of that, let us think a few minutes about this almost-strange notion of God's exalting us. Why would God even want to exalt us? When He does, how do we handle it? What do we do with it? In order to answer, we must return to the basics of the gospel—man is justified by grace alone through faith alone because of Jesus alone. In other words, man cannot be justified as the result of his own merits, nor can he be justified as the result of the exercise of his will. In other words, justification by faith cannot exist if separated from one's recognition of his own sin's exceeding sinfulness and his desperate need for the Savior—humility in its purest form. When God, through the law, drives man to this humble place of awareness and desperation before Jesus and justifies him, He does, indeed, exalt him by not only releasing him from the guilt, condemnation, power, and penalty of sin, but also by granting him sonship as a fellow heir with Jesus! I might add that this exaltation, obviously, precipitates humility, not pride.

In the end, it is impossible to understand the concepts of humility and pride without revisiting the heart and essence of the gospel—justification by grace through faith in Jesus alone. In their purest forms, pride has to do with one's attempting to contribute to his own justification by various works—*Humility and How I Achieved It*—whereas, humility has to do with resting in Jesus's finished work of redemption—*Humility and How He Achieved It*.

Humble yourself in His presence, and He will exalt you!

26

The Danger of Speaking against One Another

> "Do not speak against one another, brethren. He who speaks against a brother, or judges his brother, speaks against the law, and judges the law; but if you judge the law, you are not a doer of the law, but a judge of it. There is only one Lawgiver and Judge, the One who is able to save and to destroy; but who are you who judge your neighbor?" (James 4:11–12).

At first glance, it appears that James is telling us not to speak against one another; however, he surely does not mean for us to take his statement literally. There is this good evidence: he equates our "speaking against one another" with our "judging one another" and that places a whole new light, a new perspective, on the subject.

For example, to take the literal position that we can never speak against one another *could* be taken to mean that we can never disagree, especially in light of the fact that most of us have a very difficult time separating the undesirable behavior from the person who is carrying out the undesirable behavior.

Furthermore, taking this literal position could also be taken to mean that we can never admonish or correct one another, especially in light of the fact that most of us interpret admonishment and correction as a statement of our being less than a whole person—unaccepted, unloved, and worthless—and, therefore, unable to measure up.

In order to grasp the heart of this passage, we must understand that there is a vast difference between our speaking against another out of the desire to diminish his sense of value, love, and acceptance, and our speaking against him out of the desire to speak the truth in love. To say that another way, there is a vast difference between our speaking against a brother and, thereby, judging his standing with God, and our speaking against a brother because we are genuinely concerned and honestly care about the direction his life is taking. Not only that, we must also understand that our identity is not determined by anything another might say; rather, our identity is in Christ Jesus.

Since James equates "speaking against one another" not only with judging one another, but also with judging the law, allow me to clarify his choice and use of the verb to judge. In the original language, the word that defines "judge," as it is used in our text, is κρινω. It means to separate, to select, to choose; hence, to determine, and so to judge, pronounce judgment.[5] There are several New Testament uses of this verb: (1) to assume the office of a judge, Matthew 7:1; (2) to undergo the process of a trial, John 3:18; (3) to give sentence, Acts 15:19; (4) to condemn, John 12:48; (5) to execute judgment upon, 2 Thessalonians 2:12; (6) to be involved in a lawsuit as a plaintiff or as a defendant, Matthew 5:40.

As you can see, this is a very strong word, and when it is used in the context of the gospel, it can only have to do with our making a determination (judgment) of one's standing with God, and in this passage it has to do with our using the law to make that determination.

---

5 Vine, W.E. *An Expository Dictionary of New Testament Words*, New York: Revell, 1940.

You see, when we use the law as the standard for righteousness, we are judging it to be both a valid (legally binding) and a reliable (dependable) instrument to make such a determination—an inaccurate judgment, to say the least. So, when one believer speaks against another believer, not out of the desire to speak truth in love, but out of the desire to judge him unrighteous, he, obviously, does so using the law as the standard. In doing so, he not only speaks against the law, he also falsely judges it. As you remember, Jesus, not the law, is the standard for righteousness; consequently, to speak *for* the law is to declare its true purposes—to reveal sin, to reveal sin's exceeding sinfulness, to reveal the exceeding sinfulness of our own sin, to reveal our own helplessness, and to drive us to Jesus (see Romans 3:20, 6:23a, 7:13, and Galatians 3:19, 24).

On the other hand, to speak against the law is to present it not only as the standard for righteousness, but also as the means for righteousness. To be sure, when we so speak against it, we clearly demonstrate that we are not doers of the law but judges of it.

To be sure, there is but one lawgiver and judge—the One who not only is able to save, but also is able to destroy. Who, then, are we to judge one another?

27
Planning for the Future

"Come now, you who say, 'Today or tomorrow, we shall go to such and such a city, and spend a year there and engage in business and make a profit.' Yet you do not know what your life will be like tomorrow. You are just a vapor that appears for a little while and then vanishes away. Instead, you ought to say, 'If the Lord wills, we shall live and also do this or that.' But as it is, you boast in your arrogance; all such boasting is evil. Therefore, to one who knows the right thing to do, and does not do it, to him it is sin" (James 4:13–17).

To be honest, James's writing style can be a bit distracting, especially in light of the way he shifts from one subject to another without any warning. This passage serves as a good example because it forces my mind to wander from its focus on what appeared to be his theme, to wondering what prompted these seemingly off-the-wall comments. It seems that he ended verse 12 and left for a month's sabbatical, and when he returned he started writing about whatever was on his mind at that time. Even so, it is Holy Writ, so we should examine it.

Most of us have been taught the benefits of planning for the future; however, most of us neglected to practice what we have been taught. For example, most of us know that financial planning is a good thing, but most never make financial plans, not even a simple budget. As a result, few of us have any financial goals. The trend today is to live from paycheck to paycheck and hope for the best, oftentimes with the erroneous mind-set that says, "I am doing all I can do."

In much the same way, most of us know that spiritual planning is a good thing, but most of us never make spiritual plans; consequently, few of us have any spiritual goals. As a result, most wander aimlessly through the Christian life, wondering why the journey is so confusing and so difficult. The trend today is to live from sermon to sermon, oftentimes with the erroneous mind-set that says, "I do not have the time or the ability to dig it out for myself."

Planning is a good thing, a very good thing, and we must never be deceived into believing anything less. James, however, is making an even greater point, and it is this (said succinctly): be careful about making plans you cannot change because you have no idea what will be going on in your life tomorrow, much less next year. And you might want to remember that God probably has some plans of His own for you, plans that are diametrically opposed to yours. He goes on to tell us that our making plans without having first submitted them to Him is not only boasting, but also boasting in our arrogance, which is the epitome of foolishness.

It took me a while to understand why he closed this portion with these very haunting and familiar words: *therefore, to one who knows the right thing to do, and does not do it, to him it is sin.* However, it finally became obvious. We struggle to do what we know is the right thing to do because we have already made plans—selfish plans—to do otherwise.

What have you planned for tomorrow, for next week, for next year that will interfere with your doing what you know is the right thing to do? Remember: to know the right thing to do but refuse to do it is sin.

28

Rotten Riches, Moth-Eaten Garments, and Rusted Gold and Silver

"Come now, you rich, weep and howl for your miseries which are coming upon you. Your riches have rotted and your garments have become moth-eaten. Your gold and your silver have rusted; and their lust will be a witness against you and will consume your flesh like fire. It is in the last days that you have stored up your treasure! Behold, the pay of the laborers who mowed your fields, and which has been withheld by you, cries out against you; and the outcry of those who did the harvesting has reached the ears of the Lord of Sabaoth. You have lived luxuriously on the earth and led a life of wanton pleasure; you have fattened your hearts in a day of slaughter. You have condemned and put to death the righteous man; he does not resist you" (James 5:1–6).

Now, we all know that riches, in and of themselves, are not evil; however, we also know (and are, therefore, without excuse) that it is our lust for them that gets us into trouble. "For we have brought nothing into the world, so we cannot take anything out of it either. And if we have food and covering, with these we shall be content. But those who want to get rich fall into temptation and a snare and many foolish and harmful desires which plunge men into ruin and destruction. For **the love of**

money is a root of all sorts of evil, and some by longing for it have wandered away from the faith, and pierced themselves with many a pang" (1 Timothy 6:7–10; emphasis mine).

Mike Mason, in his book *The Gospel according to Job*, said this: "What causes a person to suffer is one of the surest indications of what it is that he or she believes in" (page 63). Obviously, it goes without saying that most of us believe in the power of riches to make us happy, as is evidenced by the amount of suffering either its presence, or the lack thereof, seems to cause us. "Come now, you rich, weep and howl for your miseries which are coming upon you" (James 5:1).

I am sure you remember the story (Luke 12:16–21) of the "rich fool" who had far more possessions than he needed, and, rather than doing the wise thing, he chose to build bigger barns in which to store his goods, so he could take his ease, eat, drink, and be merry (verse 19). God's response to him was quite unsettling: "You fool! This very night your soul is required of you and now who will own what you have prepared?" (verse 20).

I have the feeling that before he died he was very familiar with the pang, the miseries to which James alluded. You can readily see that there was nothing inherently wrong with his riches; instead, it was his lust for them, his belief in their power to make him happy, that got him into trouble—deep trouble. I wonder what God's response would have been had he chosen to use his abundance to feed the hungry, clothe the naked, and support orphans. Of this I am certain: his riches would have never rotted, his gold and silver would have never become rusty, and his garments would have never become moth-eaten! He would probably have lived long enough to see firsthand that it really is "more blessed to give than to receive" (see Acts 20:35b).

May it never be said of any of us that we *have lived luxuriously on the earth and led a life of wanton pleasure; that we have fattened our hearts in a day of slaughter* (James 5:5). Jesus's words are quite unsettling: "Woe to you who are rich, for you are receiving your comfort in full" (Luke 6:24); "It is easier for a camel to go through the eye of a needle than for a rich man to enter the kingdom of God" (Mark 10:25).

29

The Coming of the Lord Is at Hand

"Be patient, therefore, brethren, until the coming of the Lord. Behold, the farmer waits for the precious produce of the soil, being patient about it, until it gets the early and late rains. You too be patient, strengthen your hearts, for the coming of the Lord is at hand" (James 5:7–8).

Wow! James is telling us that the coming of the Lord is at hand! Since he wrote this a few hundred years ago, actually quite a few hundred years ago, I wonder what he meant. According to my concept of time, he misinformed us, to say the least (unless He came and I missed it!); however, according to God's concept of time (He is eternally now!), maybe he got it right after all, and I am just living in the wrong time zone.

Even so, let me ask you this: do you really believe that the coming of the Lord is at hand, or is it just, well, a lost hope? Peter must have anticipated this "lost hope," as is evidenced by what he had to say: "The Lord is not slow about His promise, as some count slowness, but is patient toward you, not wishing for any to perish, but for all to come to repentance. But the day of the Lord will come like a thief, in which the heavens will pass away with a roar and the elements will be destroyed with intense heat, and the earth and its works will be burned up" (2 Peter 3:9–10). To be honest, that can a bit unnerving, especially in view of what is being said today (2012) about the devastation that would result from the real possibility of someone detonating a nuke right here in the good old USA, even a very small one, one that would fit into a Ford or Chevy van.

Well, I say "a bit unnerving," and it is, but to those of us who know Him and are expecting His return, these should be the most encouraging words we could ever read. Even so, if we were certain that Jesus was going to return in the morning, we would experience quite a bit of anxiety not only regarding those who might not be among His elect, but also regarding our own fears. After all, not one of us has previously made this trip. Unnerving or not, *Jesus is coming again*, and you can depend on it, look for it, expect it, and be exceedingly glad!

Notice that James encourages us to patiently await Jesus's return, comparing our waiting to the farmer who patiently waits for the early and late rains that bring forth the "precious produce of the soil." Sadly, patience is not one of the virtues that most of us lay claim to possessing; certainly, most of us have learned the hard way *not* to ask God to give us patience!

As I see it, (which is, admittedly, somewhat clouded) most Christians are content with God taking His good time to send Jesus on His return trip, and they are because they fear the Great White Throne Judgment, the one where all their sins will be shown on a huge HD plasma screen for the entire world to see. Sadly, few seem to know that Jesus (the One who is returning!) bore their sins in His body on the cross and, thus, imputed His righteousness to them. Won't they be surprised when they discover that they have already been judged as being as righteous as Jesus is righteous? I wonder just how impatient they would become, should they learn this incredible truth. It makes me wonder if James wasn't assuming that his readers knew this truth.

I must admit, however, that there are many Christians who are impatiently (enthusiastically) awaiting Jesus's return, but for the wrong reason. They want to get out of their miserable existence on this earth and move on to whatever Heaven might be, thinking that whatever it is, it is better than what they know here. Well, they are correct in that judgment, but that is not the reason they should be eagerly awaiting Jesus's return. These folk really need a heaping helping of patience, the kind that allows them to see and to embrace the truth that Jesus came that we might have life and have it abundantly—right here on planet earth. Heaven is not our escape from misery but our entrance into that celestial city of God, where we will enjoy Him forever.

Thankfully, there are those who are impatiently waiting on His return because they simply long to see Him and to experience the consummation of the love relationship. These are the folk who need to heed James's words about our patiently waiting, and for good reason: He makes all things beautiful in His time!

Listen up: *The coming of the Lord is at hand!*

30

Is Anyone among You Suffering, Cheerful, or Sick?

> "Is anyone among you suffering? Let him pray. Is anyone cheerful? Let him sing praises. Is anyone among you sick? Let him call for the elders of the church, and let them pray over him, anointing him with oil in the name of the Lord; and the prayer offered in faith will restore the one who is sick, and the Lord will raise him up, and if he has committed sins, they will be forgiven him. Therefore, confess your sins to one another, and pray for one another, so that you may be healed. The effective prayer of a righteous man can accomplish much. Elijah was a man with a nature like ours, and he prayed earnestly that it might not rain; and it did not rain on the earth for three years and six months. And he prayed again, and the sky poured rain, and the earth produced its fruit" (James 5:13–18).

These are probably the questions James would ask today: Is there anyone among us who is not suffering? Is there anyone among us who is not depressed? Is there anyone among us who is not sick? Obviously, suffering, depression, and sickness are the norm for today's society, especially today's religious society.

Interestingly, James offers some remedies, but most modern-day (postmodern) believers do not give them much credibility, as is evidenced by the way they are ignored by the Christian community. How long has it been since you have called for the elders of your church and asked them to anoint you with oil and to pray for your healing? How long has it been since you have seen anyone follow this directive? Even more importantly, how long has it been since you have seen this directive actually work?

How long has it been since someone who was suffering came to you and asked for counsel and you responded with, "Pray!"? Yes, I know how this plays itself out; the suffering person comes to you wanting sympathy, and, instead of offering him what he needs, that which will benefit him, you offer him that he wants—sympathy. I wonder what would happen if you offered him what he really needs. This is my guess: if you should offer him what James suggests, he would perceive that you are rejecting him and, therefore, quickly reject you.

What about the depressed (which is most of the population!)? What does James offer as a remedy? You should know, as you just read it—sing praises. Now, if my guess is correct, it is very difficult to sing praises when you are depressed. I mean, who wants to sing praises to the very God who is responsible for your being depressed? Come on, James, get a clue! Asking a depressed person to sing praises is about like asking a nauseated person to eat spaghetti and meatballs! But you know the truth. If you can ever talk yourself into singing those praises, the light begins to shine, faintly at first, but shine, nevertheless. When it is dark, really dark, any light is a bright, shining light!

Then James introduces the "therefore" word: therefore confess your sins to one another! Yeah, right! Do you really think that I am going trust you enough to confess my sins to you? That will be a surefire way for the entire world to know about them, and that ain't (excuse my English!) on my list of desires.

Admittedly, I have been involved in groups where this happened to some extent, but it did not take me long to learn that the church ain't (excuse my English again!) the safest place on earth—not even close. It is a shame, but most prayer meetings, where sins are confessed, become gossip sessions, where lives are ruined.

Notice that James not only told us to confess our sins to one another, but also to pray for one another. I get the impression that he meant for us to confess our sins to one another, within the context of praying for one another. However, in my opinion, he said this without anticipating the direction that prayer meetings would take over the course of years.

He did, however, have this good purpose in mind: that we might be healed. Within this context, our praying for one another is a good thing, a very good thing, because the effective prayer of a righteous man can accomplish much. We must remember, however, that He never intended for prayer to be a tool of leverage that we could use to persuade Him to change his mind. Much to the contrary, He intended (in my opinion) for prayer to be His method of moving us to that place where we desire His will over our own, even when it involves our own sickness. When we finally arrive at this point, prayer does accomplish much! Who in their "right" mind (if anyone is) would want to change God's mind, anyway?

31

On Straying from the Truth

"My brethren, if any among you strays from the truth, and one turns him back, let him know that he who turns a sinner from the error of his way will save a soul from death, and will cover a multitude of sins" (James 5:19–20).

This passage is difficult—very difficult—especially in light of the fact that it is addressed to "My brethren." One must assume that James is not referring to his physical brothers, but to his spiritual brothers (and sisters)—i.e., those who, like James, are believers in Jesus for their redemption and salvation. Furthermore, he makes it sound like the one who "turns a sinner from the error of his way" is his savior, which we know cannot be true, nor do we believe that James thought that to be true. Yes, he can be very contrary at times, but surely that was not his position.

The fact is every believer will stray from the truth, probably more often than not, but never so much as to cause him to become a sinner in need of being saved again. Jesus's work of redemption was perfect and complete. These are His own words: "My sheep hear My voice, and I know them, and they follow

Me; and I give eternal life to them, and they shall never perish; and no one shall snatch them out of my hand. My Father, who has given them to Me, is greater than all; and no one is able to snatch them out of the Father's hand. I and the Father are one" (John 10:27–30). If that is difficult to understand, then forget trying to understand John 3:16!

In my opinion, there is nothing more arrogant than one thinking that he can somehow turn a sinner from the error of his way, and, thus, save his soul from death. That job is for the Holy Spirit, and that, my friend, is a good thing—a very good thing—if for no other reasons than the facts that (1) we make very poor judges, and (2) our blood is inadequate to save anyone from anything because the blood of bulls and goats cannot take away sin! "For it is impossible for the blood of bulls and goats to take away sins" (Hebrews 10:4). We should get out of the judging and saving business—altogether and completely!

Now, having said that, let me hasten to say that when one of God's children strays from the truth and the Holy Spirit turns him from the error of his way, back to the truth, He will certainly have done a good thing—a very good thing.

If, however, James is referring to all of the Jews who had been dispersed abroad, namely, the twelve tribes of Israel, then his text is more easily understood. "James, a bond-servant of God and of the Lord Jesus Christ, to the twelve tribes who are dispersed abroad, greetings" (James 1:1).

Most, if not all of these people, were steeped in Judaism, and their roots were near and dear to their hearts. Obeying the Torah (Law) was of utmost importance to them, even to those who had put their faith in Yeshua (Jesus) for redemption and salvation. They had no idea that Jesus, through His vicarious death, burial, resurrection, and ascension, had released them from the law. They had no idea that they were no longer slaves to that by which they had been bound. They were just beginning this journey, taking "baby steps," that for them seemed like huge, gigantic steps. James knew this; consequently, he was simply trying to keep them on board long enough to see Christ formed in them. "My children, with whom I am again in labor until Christ is formed in you" (Galatians 4:19).

Closing Comments

In my opinion, Martin Luther was spot-on when he labeled James's letter to the twelve tribes of Israel who were dispersed abroad as a book of straw. Finding the truth in this letter is much like finding a needle in a haystack. To be sure, it takes much work, the kind of work that only those who have a passion for the truth of God's Word will put forth.

To be honest, I also think it takes years of Bible study, not the kind of study one does to learn the rules for Christian living, but the kind one does in an effort to know Him whom to know is eternal life. To be sure, those who refuse to think outside the paradigm of their own experience will never discover the truth of James's letter. Only those who have the courage to set aside their theological prejudices, abandon their sacred cows, and explore the places they have heretofore refused to explore will be able to find the proverbial needle in this haystack.

It is my sincere prayer that the hours I have spent putting together my perspective on the book of James will not have been spent in vain. If you are reading this, please know that I have already prayed that the needle of truth in James's letter has pricked your heart and motivated you to press on in your passion to know Him whom to know is eternal life.

May the love of God constrain you; may the joy of the Lord be your strength, and may the peace that passes all understanding be yours in fullest measure. Amen.